A Rite of Paso :

Paso Robles Wine Country

Chris Kassel

COVER AND DESIGN BY JESSE KASSEL

Paperback Edition
First Printing 2013

Copyright © 2013 by Chris Kassel

Published by Intoxicology Press LLC

ISBN-13: 978-1494334758
ISBN-10: 1494334755

I had long entertained the idea of spending a fantasy month among the vines and wines of a single appellation, learning things that no bottle can tell you: The flickering, hands-on nuances of terroir and the dynamics behind a backstory.

I chose Paso Robles in part because I wanted a sturdy but moving target, in part because I knew little about it physically and in part because I dig what they do, how they think and the direction in which the Paso pulpit is pointing. In the end, I couldn't have chosen a better milieu or a more ferocious plot.

I visited dozens of wineries, and here, I've written about a mere handful of them. This is not a guidebook; this is not my idea of a definitive Paso opus, nor is the inclusion of some wineries meant to detract from the legacy of others, many of whom may rightly be considered icons of the AVA. I wrote about the turf that I found most intriguing and the characters I found most compelling.

Ultimately, that's all it is, of course: The people of a place – the creatures spattered across the canvas like a patina – that make a portrait indelibly richer.

- Chris Kassel, December 1, 2013

A RITE OF PASO

'When the train comes, we'll get on board...' - Springsteen,
Living Proof

The last locomotive rattled away from the train station on
West Vernor in 1988, and when you cross the Ambassador
Bridge and enter Detroit, the building's malignant shell is the
first thing you see. It's a beetling, haunted-looking husk,
defiant in death, a haven for junkies, the homeless and scene
kids with Nikons.

'King of Kings', Percy Shelley, *Mondo Metaphoro*, move it on
over. Ozymandias had nothing on Michigan Central Station,
once the tallest train depot in the world.

Around a hundred years ago, my great uncle departed from
that (then) spanking-new depot, and headed to California to
seek his fortune. I knew him at the tail end of his life, long
after he'd moved back to Detroit, and among the stories he
told me about that trip, one in particular stood out—he spoke
with awe about seeing curlews from his Pullman car window,
flocks rising from wetlands in such numbers that the skies
darkened.

I remember that story in particular because once, when he and
I were listening to a radio show together, some geeky
ornithologist was lecturing about the habits of this marvelous
bird and apparently got something wrong. My know-it-all
uncle called the station to correct him, saying that *he'd* never
witnessed a single one of the millions of curlews he'd seen act
this way.

My uncle failed to mention that he hadn't seen a curlew since World War I, and the poor bird doc nearly popped an excitement embolism, since the species is believed to be extinct.

Well, the curlews are gone, my uncle is gone, and by mid-September, 2013 I'm just as gone. Detroit to California by rail, albeit under different circumstances and for a whole different set of reasons.

On these, I have no reason to dwell, but they require a mention, because they drive the direction, focus, selfishness and suppositions — the Ozymandias-quality arrogance — of what I'm trying to carry off. After two decades of spectacularly embarrassing, physically damaging and frequently ridiculous drinking, I had pretty much dinged or destroyed most of my loves and friendships; two marriages and countless colleagues, kin and seven kids who had stood guard when I probably needed it and several of whom drank with me when I probably didn't.

My leaving was a brain wring; not unilateral, but mutual; fully agreed to by those I affect, those who affect me, and who, by the essential daisy-chain of emotion, will continue to travel with me in affection and affectation — good and bad — until the end of days. Leaving for a long time is maybe not the best solution, but even dry and humbled, it's the only one.

A train because it's symbolic, of course; California because on a westbound carrier, it's the end of the line. Plus, it's where the wine is, and if I should not — cannot — drink any more of it, I have spent my entire adult life writing about wine, millions of words in dozens of outlets, and writing about wine and wine's inhabitants is still my comfort zone, even when the comfort zone of a low-grade buzz is no longer an option.

A non-drinking drunk throwing himself into a vat of syrah and thinking he can float, not drown, is perhaps where the presumptions of Ozymandias must come to the surface or sink forever.

And Paso Robles, midway between San Francisco and Los Angeles, in part because that's where Bridget is. I met Bridget after my second divorce and then as now, she represents things that are cleansing, wholesome and pure. We have talked about fusing, about marriage; we have owned that there is a parallel universe of maybes, and even if the concept itself is a maybe, when the train comes, we get on board.

As the Wolverine pulls away from the ratty little Detroit train station — no more than a Plexiglas bus stop — I realize that there are automotive guys sitting behind me and they are sputtering on about ISO audits, spuming over the cost of money, cash flow positives. I listen with equal parts revulsion and sympathy; they sound like they care about this crap, but I believe that these are the lives of quiet desperation that Thoreau wrote about; it's the company front. I believe this because I spent twenty years in the car industry talking exactly like these dorks — the day job that not only allowed me to write about wine, but forced me to write about wine (or anything else not made of steel and polypropylene) as mental fumigation to purge the carbon monoxide — that ol' Detroit perfume — after the five o'clock whistle blew. I fled that world at a near opportune moment, which is to say, right before my requisite, inevitable and total self-implosion.

As creepy as the automotive guys are, there is something ineffably comforting about the train's conductor; retro cap, neat red necktie, avuncular smile and gentle tone. I've never known a flight attendant that didn't seem to be trying a little too hard, although in her defense, of course, a conductor has less concern that his day will end with a terrorist driving the

Wolverine into a skyscraper.

I am seated with Kari, a Hamtramck girl in camouflage overalls; she is strikingly beautiful if you can overlook copious armpit hair, multiple tattoos and piercings, which you somehow can. Kari's engaging; she's on her way to Montana to spend the autumn operating huge machines in the sugar beet field — seasonal work for which she will earn enough scoot that upon returning, she'll be able to pay off her mortgage.

Vaya con Dios; buena suerte, Kari.

Dawn pokes up over central Michigan with opaque ribbons of fog hovering at second story level; pine spires surface from the mist with coral crowns; the fog clears amid stands of trees showing splats of brilliant red — maples giving the ghost up early. But human intervention is already blighting these bucolic morning vistas; scrapyards with cars smashed into blocks and piled into fences, smokestacks billowing sputum, abandoned Conrail cars splayed with spray-paint tags, Crankshaft Machine company, karaoke bars, 'Leasing Specials' signs on apartments a hundred yards from the tracks that you know you'd regret leasing at any price the first morning the first Amtrak blasted by.

These are worn-out little towns and they spackle the Midwest like jetsam, failing, forlorn, forgotten, losing populations at rates of 5% per census. This does not quell the enthusiasm of our animated conductor, who announces the approach of each one with a clever nickname, offering some tidbit of ancient history.

There's Mendota, *'The Best Little Town in America'*, where the tallest municipal feature is a water tower so poorly maintained that you can't read 'Mendota' through the rust.

Picturesque Princeton, *'That Perfect Little Midwest Town'* is dusty and forgotten; the land of Rotary Club-donated park benches and piles of obsolete pallets and unreclaimable tires, billed by our narrator as an *'Internet Hotspot'*, whatever that means.

Greater Galesburg is *'The Fine Railroad Town'*, a whistle-stop for Abraham Lincoln when he was campaigning; the site of the third Douglass/Lincoln debate in 1858 and, according to the conductor, *'the spot where the Marx Brothers received their nicknames'*. No further explanation is offered; he's reading from a cue card.

Outside Fort Madison, we're urged to watch out for a llama farm, as if that's best thing the town can come up with as a tourist draw. Alas, the llamas are all indoors this afternoon, and seeing the moony faces of the curious at the Observing Car window, the llama farmer, for reasons known but to him, flips us the bird.

And so on. In 1966, each of Paul Simon's *Homeward Bound* towns looked the same, and today they still do, except that the movie theaters are now shuttered and the factories are windowless and festooned with graffiti.

Between them are amber waves — nay, amber tsunamis — of grain. Corn, now in its seasonal dotage, consume vast tracts, far more today than when *Simon & Garfunkel* were playing the small town circuit.

But as the sun goes down over the Mississippi River, America's natural beauty reasserts herself, turning the water powder blue above a dunnish tree line, with pink clouds rising beyond as a burgeoning, buoyant bank of mountains.

On a westbound train, if you fall asleep in a pastoral grain belt of green and gold, you awaken in an alien world of desolate red soil and anemic scrub. It's a transmutation so remarkable that you're never really able wrap your head around it, no matter how many times you experience it.

I've done this trip a half dozen times by car and I am always amazed at how flat Colorado is before the Rockies do their *carpe diem*. I have no doubt that the wagon train families had the same unnerving thought: *Where the hell are the mountains?*

And when they finally do appear as stains in the distance, ominous and mirage-like, it is easy to imagine the sense of foreboding that must have settled over those unimaginably poor, ineffably courageous pioneer families. And they had days before them — maybe weeks — to dwell upon the horizon as the stains gradually became dark and featureless ribbons, and the ribbons became angry upheavals from which many of them would not — and knew they would not — emerge.

Some time during the night, several Amish families have boarded the train, and in all my insular urban naïveity this surprises me because I thought that Amish people weren't allowed to ride trains, or anything that had a motor running it. So there goes the old joke, 'What goes clip-clop, clip-clop, *bang!?* An Amish drive-by'. I'm embarrassed to ask, and even more embarrassed when I finally do and an old matriarch explains to me that not only can the Amish ride trains, they can drive tanks or Corvettes or own wide-screen televisions or operate John Deere S-Series harvester combines — but they choose not to. Because she wears an expression halfway between weary forbearance and annoyed mind-your-own-businesses, I'm a little put off, although later on, when the lot of them have their noses stuck in Bibles, I manage to refrain from saying, "Haven't you finished that damn thing *yet?*"

A young father is traveling with his son, about four years old, and here's a hint for parents who do not want to hear some pre-school variation on *The Wheels on the Train Go Round and Round* for seven hundred straight miles: Forget the song exists and do not under any circumstance teach it to your kid.

Mid-life-crisis Brock has been seated across the aisle from me since Chicago, when Kari hopped off to head north to bulldoze beets and I switched from the Wolverine line to the Southwest Chief. Brock tells me that he paid seventeen hundred dollars for a sleeper car, then met an extremely pregnant hooker in Chicago's Union Station lobby who was heading home to Albuquerque hoping to get her life back on track; he felt bad for and gave her some money for which she offered him a blowjob, which he declined, and now tells me he is riding coach while she sleeps in his bed.

Who knows? He's one of those guys who crank-raps without requiring methamphetamine, but telling him to shut up is the sort of bad karma rude that I plan to avoid on this trek. Besides, his stories are sort of fascinating, if likely figmental: He confides that three weeks ago in a drunken soul-search he wandered out into the prairie and built a sweat lodge, where he remained for thirty-nine hours. He must have still been shit-faced when he emerged, because he claims to have accidentally left several thousands dollars worth of items — jewelry, cell phone, wrist watch — in a pile next to the lodge and, now he's signed The Pledge and is on his way back to try to find them. He detrains at La Plata.

Vaya con Dios; buena suerte, Brock.

He's replaced by an old, old black man in open-toed sandals who has managed to get lost on the train and plops down for a breather, long enough to pound his chest and bark 'Kalamazoo!' when he hears me give a Michigan address over the cellphone.

He proceeds to advise me, 'Call me Bebop'. And, as we are

rolling past cattle pasture, he shares an odd nonsequitur:

*'I was in a valley down in Texas once?   And the road was blocked
by a thousand head of Longhorns — maybe two thousand.
Thousands, anyway. The methane from their assholes made a fog so
thick that it filled the whole damn valley, the whole damn valley, and
nobody could drive for the stank...'*

That day — if he was indeed from Kalamazoo — Bebop learned
what my uncle had learned: There's dimensions to things out
West of which those of us from the hyper-compacted East
cannot conceive. The conductor comes to escort him back to
his seat and I assure Bebop that he's my kind of storyteller:
Get in, tell the thing and scram.

Travel safely, Bebop. Good luck.

We have an hour to kill in Albuquerque, and even though my
father lives there, I fail to call him for private reasons that
could fill another book if I cared to write it. But I don't,
because the subject needs nothing beyond the thing my pal
Laura shook her head and said as she watched her brother go
through the same phenomenon many years ago: *'Fathers and
sons...'*

See, those three words are the title of the book, the whole text
and all of the sequels.

But through the window, as I watch the handful of people
who are leaving the train, I note that among them there is a
ponderously pregnant young woman in a too-short skirt who
looks confused, abandoned and frightened.

Godspeed, hooker. May more Brocks be in your future.

Another incident-free night passes, except for the cigarette
stop we make in Winslow, Arizona. I jump off the train, not

to smoke, not to leg-stretch, but to do what I've done every time I've been through this podunk, touchstone town since I was a teenager: I stand on a corner. If you've glommed onto the '70's rock motif I've somehow fallen into, you'll get that without explanation.

In Los Angeles, I swap the Southwest Chief for the Coast Starlight, which hugs the Pacific Ocean from Oxnard to San Luis Obispo and is probably quite lovely by starlight. It is, however, the middle of the afternoon and stupendously hot.

For this final journey leg, I'm seated with Emiliano, a migrant picker from Michoacán who is also heading to Paso Robles for the wine, although in his case, it's to harvest the grapes that make it. He tells me that he's worked crop fields since he was eight years old, when he earned a few dollars a week picking strawberries; from there, he graduated to sugar cane, and displays his brutal brown palms with pride and resignation; they're criss-crossed with scars from the technology-free techniques still in use in Mexican cane agriculture. It's clear to see why he's opted to head north, where he will earn five hundred dollars for a fifty hour work week in the vineyards, nearly all of which he will send to his wife and three kids in Michoacán. He looks fifty, but he's probably thirty-five. I buy him a coffee from the café and he gives me tamale that his nephew made the night before when he stopped to see him in Los Angeles. I get the better end of the stick. We part company as the train pulls into the station at Paso Robles; I take his calloused, damaged grip in my spongy, white boy palm and wish him luck, laughter and love throughout his tour of life's art and excrement.

And now we're here. *Buena suerte* yourself, Kassel. Go with the gods of wine and reconfiguration.

THE VERY PINK OF COURTESY: STILLMAN BROWN

Of all silly places, I met Bridget on Facebook: These are the best of times, these are the worst of times.

She's supposed to be here to scoop me from the depot, but has been delayed a long way outside of town by a traffic accident, and the span of time I end up waiting winds up being a sort of a godsend. I have learned, somewhere along the train route, that the roommate Bridget spoke about when I was sussing out Paso hostels wherein to sleep, turns out to be something a bit more substantial. She has, in fact, a live-in squeeze, making a nightly couch crash rather out of the question.

That's cool, and an eventuality for which I had prepared — by which I mean I brought along a tent and a sleeping bag. But in the time I spend on the wooden bench in front of the depot, with all the small-town serendipity of a Capra film, the dude with whom I will wind up spending much of the next four weeks rolls up in a rented 14-foot Ford F-350 filled with wooden pallets.

"Welcome to the People's Republic of Paradise," Stillman Brown bellows through the rolled-down window. *'E-Cigarettes is watching you. I'm the first person to meet you in Paso, so let me the first to dump you."*

And off he rumbles in his U-Haul.

But I see from the git-go that Stillman Brown will serve this story like Ishmael did his, Like Pip did his, like that moldering, mewling mofo from *Tales From The Crypt* served his.

'Swilly' to friends, Stillman Brown doesn't epitomize the

rough, tumble frontline winemakers of Paso Robles, except that he does. He's not the embodiment of bootstraps, hardscrabble agriculturists who take a week to drill through stone to plant a handful of vines, except that he is. By noon the following afternoon, renting my own transportation — an ugly Enterprise Dodge — I've made my way from Paso Robles to Stillman's house in Morro Bay, a touristy town perched on the ocean called 'The Gibraltar of the Pacific' thanks to the incongruous, Jujube-shaped volcanic pustule that pokes from the bay. It's a pretty, pricey and personable town, and Stillman plans to die there if he can afford to live there that long.

Tightly wound, with an umbilical fuse that seems directly attached to an adult beverage, Stillman Brown makes high-wattage wine. His wines can be cheeky and epic, enveloping and huge, cadenced and concerted, and when he wins a competition it is often by a vast margin. But in Paso Robles, as I will soon learn, it is gauche to get too infatuated with contest medals — it brands you an outsider. Drooling over Robert Parker Jr. scores is the sort of fashion *faux pas* that's hard to live down — that's the kind of fail that people with law degrees and collapsible bikes make.

Although — in fairness — the one and only hundred point wine ever awarded in Paso Robles, Saxum, is acknowledged begrudgingly as 'pretty kick-ass stuff — beautifully balanced, but even so, on balance, bottled politics.

Derailing demagogues and denouncing divinity is one of Paso Robles' core competencies. In fact, many Paso winemakers claim they wouldn't let Robert Parker Jr. near their winery if it was on fire and he was carrying the world's last water bucket. Similar slurs are aimed at a certain West Coast editor whose name I will not utter beyond saying he is (and will remain) double-plus uncool to these hardcore mavericks no matter how many tattoos he gets; memories are long and this fellow once interviewed a local cabernet sauvignon maker—a good one—and asked, rhetorically, "So, are your cabs as good as those from Napa?", which struck said winemaker as a question on the idiocy level of asking Banksy if he's as good as Dali. *It pretty much depends on the qualifier, fuck you very much.*

Fair to say that around here, such hifalutin' slights linger in the hearts and minds, and fester as ferociously as within any old-school Mexican patron.

Although he's happy to rage against the party machine in general, most of Stillman's scorn is reserved for Parker Jr., probably because Parker's people once sued him—and Stillman still doesn't understand why.

The rest of us do, however: In a burst of impulsive, seemed-like-a-good-idea at the time bravado, the then-relatively-unknown winemaker dressed up a bottle of 1987 Red Zeppelin wine—itself a parody of Randall Graham's Cigare Volant Rhone blend—with a neck label that had Parker's highly-stylized image on it above the words, 'The Emperor Has No Nose'. Recently immortalized in *The Emperor of Wine* by Elin McCoy, like Queen Victoria, Parker Jr. was, suffice to say, not amused.

Incidentally, Randall Graham—among winedom's most literate provocateurs, who seems to have a sense of humor about everything except himself—sued him too.
How much of Stillman's Parker pranging is, to further overuse an already overused and unforgivably bad pun, sour grapes? How much of what he says is true and how much is kvetching? Probably about the same proportion as anything else anyone says ever. Some is accurate, no doubt, because everyone loves owning the night wherever it falls. A well-known writer recognizing the stylistic quality for which Stillman and his vinting brethren strive to master (and once mastered in one vintage, to duplicate it the next) has to be

soul-killing when its not forthcoming and inexpressibly gratifying when it is, no matter who the kudos come from or what the venue is. And one deep truism among our social species is that it is hard to dislike someone who likes you. But seriously, for me, in the end it's more fun to hear about a specific wine given a high score because everyone local knew that the critic liked the vintner's wife's tits; that psycho-specific schmoozing often translates to unearned points and that *real* winemakers—i.e., those who know *Wine Enthusiast* and *Wine Spectator's* picks and preferences so well that they don't even bother sending samples, but instead, send letters stating, *'I just released my 2010 Estate Syrah. It's worth 89 points on your scale. Thank you'*—are not intimidated by Realpolitik reviews written by people to whom the power to influence buying habits is more intoxicating than the product they're reviewing.

On the San Luis Obispo coast, there's a seedy little Witness-Protection-Program-looking town called Cayucos, five miles long and five blocks deep.

It is inhabited in the main by a menagerie of insular party animals, conservatives without Right Wing agendas, zealots without dogma, and a lot of them hang out at a raucous, rocking, ridiculous, archetypal saloon on North Ocean Avenue.

Within, the floors are crazy with the detritus of history and the walls are painted with faux-Remington cowboy clichés and you can get a drink called *'The Stillman'*. It's made with Malibu Coconut, Stoli Vanilla, Gatorade X Factor (you can substitute Red Bull without hurting or helping anything) and maraschino cherry juice. It doesn't matter what proportions you pour, because no matter how you make it, it sucks.

But it is pink. And really, not just *any* pink, but a very specific sort of fuchsia fusion which Stillman calls 'eno-psychodelic' but which at the close of the day, when all is said and the cows come home and the piper is paid and the fat lady sings, is pink.

As is Stillman. Pink socks, pink tie-dyed chef's pants, rodeo shirt emblazoned with pink hearts on the front and 'Cowgirl' in pink stitching on the back. Because he is just similar enough to everyone else in San Luis Obispo county to be endearing and just eccentric enough to be intriguing, he's the guy who knows everybody and who everybody knows — the guy who stoops to kiss the Pope's ring finger and the whole college of Cardinals and Bishops turn to each other and say, *'Who's the dude that Stillman is kissing?'*

Not that Stillman kisses dudes — even dudes with the ear of God. Which is why the odd genre of straight/non-straight humor — replete with fellatio gags (pun) and dog dick double entendres — is the endless Stillman *joke du jour*, and why his tongue-in-cheek (another pun) response to a serious, curious customer who once asked him what he did before becoming a winemaker, which was 'Gay porn', still bounces around these hallowed and somewhat illiberal hills as legend.

There's no raw like rural raw, and you'd better get used to the sluicegate of sexual, scatological and near sociopathic innuendo that hovers above everything like fruit flies over a phallic banana.

If you're the type that tends to get jittery when a three hundred pound death metal shredder remarks that he 'don't like being on the bottom', you'd be advised learn to chuckle and process such comments very, very quickly.

It's why Stillman Pink is less a puzzle than a porchful of personality paraphernalia; why a cheeba-chuffin' hard guy living the relatively hard life of a Paso wine frontiersman has a pedicurist who paints his toenails sea foam green and who custom tie-dyes his pants in a style which he calls, with grim pride, 'Not *Grateful Dead*' and who jury-rigs his broken seatbelt with electric pink duct tape — God knows where he found the stuff.

You simply absorb this crap, right? Like the Elvis stuff; another deadpan Stillman Brown soul-definer. You can ask him a hundred times why everything surrounding him is all Graceland all the time, coasters to posters, and still wind up shaking your head and going for a hundred and one. I mean, we all appreciate Elvis, but to me, living in a house with Elvis sculptures, Elvis *'The King Lives'* guitar clocks, Elvis wine caddies, Priscilla Presley's biography on the coffee table, an Elvis impersonator posing with Stillman photo on the bookshelf, a massive over-the-hearth painting of Elvis dying on the toilet, is like digging the holidays so much you never take down your Christmas tree.

He has one — and only one — divergent wall hanging, a painting of an avant garde skull, and a lame New Yorker cartoon might show an urban couple standing before it saying, 'I dunno. I just don't *see* Elvis.'

Zeppelin iconography is something else that appears to have — somewhere along the line — snagged on Stillman's neo-cortex like a non-extractable fishhook, but more on that in a trice.

First, en route to a check of the two tons of pinot noir that he has bubbling in open-top T-bins at the Paso Robles Wine Services, Stillman has an appointment at the Cayucos hair salon, which is right across the street from the Cayucos cowboy bar, which is right across the street from Schooner's and Skipper's and just down from avenue from The Sea Shanty and a couple other business that have pirated a nautical theme and been entirely keelhauled by it.

The salon is no exception, and it must be the only beauty parlor in the cosmos that looks like it was decorated by Captain Hook. Yet there it is, in the front window of the Cayucos Barber Shop: A four-foot, handmade, hand-carved model of the U.S. Constitution, only slightly damaged when the owner's grandmother ran it over while learning to drive (or, so says the placard); inside, there's museum display of wooden wheel helms, buoys and various pieces of disassembled boat on the walls with antique tin featuring Fearless Fosdick advertising Wild Root Cream Oil Hair Tonic. In fact, The Cayucos Barber Shop might have been a charming set piece for Mayberry's Floyd Lawson, except here the stylists are sizzly hot and wear leopard print miniskirts and are stippled by bod mods, multiple tats and piercings.

But like Floyd's joint, the shop sees a steady stream of locals stopping in to jaw, nosh, be shorn, and to share the communal idealism and pessimism of hamlet habitating, and although the day job talk may revolve around tuna trolling and crab trap limits and ways to hit aldehyde with sulphur so that it binds and drops out (Stillman territory), the effect is the same here as it is in every georgic farming town and forgotten fishing ville everywhere.

Stillman's mission today is a prequel to his upcoming birthday bash, an annual see-and-be-seen soirée of which I have pored over photographs for years.
This is when the day-to-day outrageousness out-punts the coverage and goes for the real deal, some of which may not be suitable for a family wine book. And this requires a certain due diligence, of course, starting with Mattie dying Stillman's hair what Vidal Sassoon might call 'platinum ice' but which a wine man knows is closer to 'oxidized viognier'. It's not quite 'clown orange' and it's not quite not, but in any case, it serves as a further inexplicable transmutation of a character who

would glow with radioactive glory in Key West, in China's Kowloon Walled City, in Greenwich Village's or Haight Ashbury's and Tottenham Court Road's hardcore heyday. In dusty, podunk California, he's a head-turner for sure, but the heads that turn mostly belong to the shoobies.

Alexis is all for it — in fact, Stillman's demure and delphic damsel, native of cajun Lafayette, insists upon it. Once or twice a year, come hell or high ceremony, she has him burned a burnished blonde. And as he stops to preen at the small thrift shop she manages in Morro Bay, the do 'n' dye is all good and he's lavished with a lotta Louisiana love. Like all self-respecting flowers of Southern womanhood, she has creative composition in her soul, but she shoos it off, referring to me as a 'real writer', which means, of course, that she's as benighted as she is beautiful.

On the way out, we run into Stillman's friend Nicole, who's up the spout, due to give birth in March, and it's fitting, because a half hour later we are sitting at the docks at the Morro Bay Estuary, shooting shit with Nicole's baby daddy Joe aboard his temporary Pelican Bay fishing boat.

Joe has more skin ink that that dude in the Bradbury novel and according to lore has a vampirette on his inner thigh and a pair of bite marks tattooed on his tallywhacker. I have no independent knowledge to confirm or deny this rumor.

Joe is a combination commercial captain and bass player for the local powerpop punk band *The Berzerks* and he knows as much about and Alembic five strings and outriggers as Stillman does about cross-flow filters, but apparently, somewhat less about great white sharks (which locals call 'the men in the gray suits'), since shortly after Nicole called him with the good news about her pregnancy, the telltale dorsal fin which had been circling his boat suddenly reared and attacked Joe's polystyrene float in a monumental display of wasted energy, and that's the story he told people on the phone that morning just before the one about his new baby.

Anyway, that boat sank and he's now skippering a smaller one and fishing much nearer shore, mostly for Dungeness crab and rock cod, which leaves him plenty of time to jam at Morro Door.

We'll get to Morro Door in a bit, like we'll wind up getting to everywhere in south central California sooner or later while lollygagging within the Stillman Brown live-wire good life.

But first, business before pleasure—even contingent, contact pleasure. Stillman is homesick for the home-away-from-home and he's sick of it, so we take a rakehell detour to Paso Robles Wine Services.

PINOT IN PASO:
CRUSHIN' ON THE QUEEN

Paso Robles Wine Services is a custom crush facility off Highway 46 east which serves winemakers like Stillman who have no brick and mortar wineries; it leases footprint space for barrels and bulk storage as well as full-service wine processing, from juicing to label-preparation filing preparation and final bottling. Between a quarter and a third of Paso Robles wine is produced like this, in one of several such facilities.

Today the mission of the *métier* is the progress of the fermentation of Stillman's pinot noir — which will wear the Stillman Brown logo — and the vigor of the secondary, malolactic fermentation of the viognier, which will wear Michael Gill Cellars'.

Malolactic fermentation is as an interesting a phenomenon to wine drinkers as it is to winemakers, even if they've never heard of it. It's what puts 'buttery' into tasting notes and is essentially a bacterial de-acidification of wines following the initial yeast fermentation. It happens either naturally or via the specific inoculation of *Oenococcus oeni* into the must, and is a process through which one of the two major grape acids, malate — a dicarboxylic acid — is converted to the other one, lactate — a monocarboxylic acid.

In laymen's terms, this means that tart, often metallic tasting malic acid (the kind found in Granny Smith apples) is chemically altered, becoming the kinder, gentler lactic acid (the kind found in mama's mammaries — hence, the word 'lactating').

It is encouraged in wine for two reasons — to decrease acidity and to promote complexity, and it is discouraged in wine for the same two reasons.

Generally, cooler climate wine grapes produce malic in quantities that may dominate the palate and upset the wine's final balance, and in these cases, a winemaker usually opts to subject at least a portion of the wine to a malolactic process.

It's used primarily in full-bodied red wines and medium-bodied whites (like Gill's viognier); the exception to prove the rule, of course, is riesling, which requires un-manipulated fruit acidity to make it sing. Riesling is, therefore, rarely (if ever) malo-mellowed and is often treated with lyzome to prevent such an about-face from happening accidentally; that's why malicky 'green apples' instead of lacticky 'butterscotch' is a common riesling descriptor.

The sporadic downside of malo is the sudden spread of the wrong kind of lactic acid bacteria, especially certain unsympathetic *Lactobacillus* strains which add strange, rodent-like aromas to white wines and a chewing-on-tinfoil wince to reds and sometimes the scent of sauerkraut as well — all obvious flaws. The promulgating profligate is 2-acetyl-3,4,5,6-tetrahydropyridine, and it is also responsible for notes of popcorn and corn chips that may show up as a non-volatile aftertastes in a malolactic wine gone wild.

None of this has happened to Stillman's Gill's viognier; at least, not so far. He pops the stopper on a pair of 225-liter neutral *limousin* barrels and lays his ear to the bunghole like an Indian scout listening to railroad tracks to hear the kinetics of an approaching train. The sound of malolactic fermentation is faint, but it is there: A slight hissing deep within the fathomage of the cooperage. So all's well.

Next, we move to the pinot noir, about which, for a whole lot of consecutive closed-car hours, I have heard Stillman mutter to himself about with the metaphysical unease of a Beckett monologue. Mastur-babbling is another of Stillman personality traits (or pathological anomalies, depending on your capacity for humor): He talks to himself pretty steadily, as though the rubber washer on the valve seat between his brain and tongue has worn out, and everything he thinks, he says. It really doesn't bother me, because it beats the heck out of listening to the steady ting of the Scion's seatbelt indicator, which still doesn't work despite the heavy pink duct tape binding.

Incidentally, for reasons known only to God, fools and little children, Stillman's car is not Elvis's Series-60 Cadillac pink. It's *Blue Christmas* blue.

There's plenty of techno-talk in Stillman's dilemma, but it boils down to this:

He bought these grapes for a not-insubstantial sum from a vineyard owner so near the ocean that the grapes received an almost perfect balance of daytime heat and nighttime cool throughout the growing season — table stakes for this Burgundian fuss-budget variety. Diaphanous and dainty from vineyard to vat, pinot noir was born with a thin skin, making it hypersensitive to weather and prone to viruses like leaf roll and bunch rot. It's recalcitrant in handling and as difficult to vinify as it is to farm; it has, as a result, often been described in feminine terms, including 'voluptuous', 'high-maintenance', 'delicate and driven to drama', 'seductive, wily and sexy'. Of course, as the French — who have been growing pinot noir since Jesus had milk teeth — well know, the better it is, the harder it is to describe. One thing is for sure: If pinot noir is a woman, it is Carla Bruni compared to cabernet sauvignon's Kim Kardashian.

Speaking of France, in Burgundy's Côte-d'Or — pinot noir's ostensible birthplace — the grapes usually see harvest parameters of 24°-25° Brix ('Brix' is a winemaker scale used to indicate sugar content), often less, which ferments out to about 15% alcohol-by-volume at the upper end. Stillman's pinot noir, a hefty Morey-Saint-Denis clone known as '777', favored for its intensity of fruit and early ripening, sits in the primary fermenters at more than 27.1° Brix. That means that it has a potential alcohol-by-volume pushing 17% alcohol, a burn approaching the oomph of Port. Even for the often high-octane wines of hot Paso Robles, where 18% alcohol is possible thanks to beefed-up yeast strains (fortified wines rely on added liquor rather than juggernaut fermentation), Stillman knows instinctively that his super-ripe pinot noir needs a bit of dilution.

And his instincts are usually right. The deal is, it's pinot noir, and it is really, really good pinot noir, and has been demonstrated again and again by hapless hacks through history, pinot noir likes to be pampered, not teased. Ergo, the problem which he's been chattering about for the last two days, to himself, to his cigar, to me, to the sea breeze that fires the wind turbines on a pass above town: When, and how much water to add.

Not what kind of water, of course; filtered water is a given, since spigot spume contains all sort of nasty undesirables you do not want in your bottled product. Like chlorine, for starters, which will at best contaminate flavors and at worst lead to cork taint.

Calcium salts, nitrates, chloramines, fluorides — even microorganisms? All in there.

For a winemaker, the bigger bugaboo is that, along with diluting the concentration of sugars, you'll also be watering down your TA, or total acidity, and in this case, the grapes came in with a pH of 3.51, and this is exactly where it is supposed to be. So, adding water will cause that number to drop along with the °Brix, requiring the addition of commercial tartaric acid to keep everything in balance.

And again, to be truly top shelf (Stillman's sole goal), pinot noir does not like to jacked around, and it is sort of an anathema to be shoring up beautiful fruit with chemicals merely to dodge bullets from cranky critics and consumers who are increasingly conscious of elevated ABVs.

It winds up being a decision tough enough that Stillman can't make it, at least not then and there, not without further muttering and sputtering. Required, evidently, is a brain dump and an acidulating-the-adjustment recalibration with a couple of R&R hours at Morro Door.

CONCEALED, THE LORD OF MORDOR SEES ALL

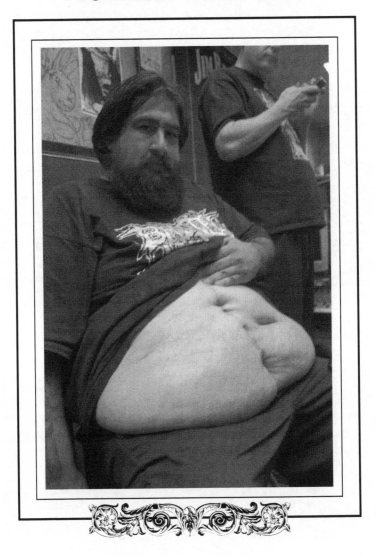

Showing off the scar will bum Rudy out, Stillman warns, but it is still something which one must gaze upon in person to truly fathom—one of those train wrecks of modern medicine that once seen, cannot be unseen.

Prior to that shadowed display of contracted tissue and purplish suture scarring, I had heard the hallowed place-name 'Morro Doors' bounced around by a lot of people I ran across. And, being too cool for school, I didn't want to ask what it was, because I figured that anybody trying to 'fit in' to this area, to navigate the social seas even for a few weeks, should already know this kind of shit. Naturally, I assumed it was a name-play on 'Mordor', because it had all sorts of dark and desperate connotations attached to it every time someone brought it up.

What I didn't figure, in all my silly speculation, was that Morro Doors really is a Morro Bay door company.

Indeed, although the website could use a quick mathematical overhaul, *'Morro Doors has been here since 1984...that's 25 years!'*, the custom provider of residential door, frames and finished lumber shelving is a respected and venerable small business on Main Street, Morro Bay's Champs-Elysees.

It's in one of the outbuildings, not in the showroom, that the tragi-comedy occurs.

By tragi-comedy, of course I mean thrasher-overload, dank-fueled, amped-up, tweaker-twisted, sequestered-in-the-dark-a-block-from-surfer's-turf bad-ass metalcore tragi-comedy.

Is there any other kind?

Crossing into the music studio, a threshold not unlike Ephel Dúath except for all the Wildhorse cigarette smoke, I find that there's an involuted wake going on.

It's been a long, long wake, I'm told, accompanied by all the maudlin micro-drama, internecine squabbling, moping and sorrow-chasing shit-facery that frequently follows a death.

But in this case, it isn't a human death — it is the passing of a neighborhood musical icon called *Meth Leppard*. The grinding, dark, three-lead-guitar humor/horror metal band recently dismantled after the emotional dismantlement of their drummer (what in the old days was called a 'nervous breakdown' is today rumored to be heroin overload) and although a bucket-banging replacement drummer seems like it should be the work of an hour or two, there are clearly deeper interpersonal bonds at work. So, between beers and bongs and blunts the size of bananas, the survivors do not audition recruits, they don't put up 'drummer wanted' ads, they don't retreat, surrender, toss in towels; they mourn, they mope, they jam.

And while Stillman goes through whatever mental gymnastics a winemaker does to decide whether to pour water into the T-Bin this afternoon or tomorrow morning, there's not much else to do but listen.

To folks like me — an audience for which this guttural and grating genre is neither directed nor intended — a superficial eavesdrop shows little more than random riffs, false cord growls punctuated by banshee cat wails, distorted overdriven leads played with arms bruised by tattoos and generally, it manifests a lot of too loud loudness.
But that's the fun of it, and maybe it's no fun, and maybe

that's the point, but in playing various musical instruments non-proficiently for many years, I did nail down some essential music theory, and if you can let the brain pain subside and mop up the ear blood, the *Meth Leppard* triple guitar interplay is built on harmonies that are remarkably intricate.

The compositions well-conceived, and if you can find funny in a perverse and goofy ode to Whitney Houston called *Lay Down And Die*, there is an aura of sophisticated irony that I swear elevates these dope-driven sounds past what a first pass suggests. That is primarily down to Rudy, or so I sense. He seems to be the nerve center, the cohesion, the locus of the studio, even though his band mate Ryland owns it. Or, as owner of the whole Morro Doors compound, which includes the jam room, Ryland's dad — also a musician — does. But, seated on his ratty recliner at the vertex of the vortex, the spasms of action, surrounded by *Motörhead* banners, *Grand Theft Auto* posters, aperçus of twats and cocks, a strange, bottomless well of graffiti, much of which may be stream-of-consciousness lyrics ('*Ass, Satan or Speed; No One Dies For Free*') and stacks upon stacks of stage equipment — expensive, beat-up speaker heads (at least one of which was purchased on a whim by one of Stillman's silver-spoon supporters), Line 6 pedals, mixing boards, congas, Rudy's prized Jackson Rhoads guitar with humbuckers — Rudy looks very much like the monarch of what he surveys. Like Elvis Presley at the tail end of things (atrocious pun, if you must drag that motif back into it): Rudy is now the age that the King was when imploded on his own throne.

According to the Bible, King Solomon's throne was made of ivory and had six steps with carved lions on each. Rudy's is made of naugehyde and his lions are a posse of hardcore, talented motherfuckers.

That's because Rudy has cinderblock gravitas — the kind that makes other axmen, no matter how 'roided and raged, unable to keep up. The kind that puts the 'ape' in apricot and makes the dawn come up like thunder.

He's nearly twice as old as some of his band mates and a whole lot fatter. With his shock of coal-black hair keeping half of his face in permanent eclipse and a raven's nest beard taking care of the other half, he gets your attention even before he picks up the Jackson Rhoads and starts to shred. When he does — playing with manic intensity, profane poise and irrefutable smarts — you either step aside or play along.

Though oddly, this whole thing began with Rudy, at ten years old, stepping away from the chops.

He comes from a musical family, for sure, but not this kind of music. At ten, he was encouraged to join a *tres* band with his uncles Joe, Henry and Ricardo; this is an extremely disciplined Latin-influenced charro music that may feature those big three-course, six-string chordophones that are said to be a physical fusion of the guitar, the tiple and the bandola. Whatever the origin, Rudy not only hated it, but also claimed that he did not show the slightest aptitude for it, eventually breaking all the strings on his guitar but one, which he continued to practice on anyway. But not *Son Jalisciense* tunes; even at tender ten Rudy was hearing riffs inside his auditory cortex a world and a culture away from his upbringing. He hears them to this day, often obsessing on them mentally for an entire week before actually playing them.

So, Rudy is the guy with the gargantuan scar on his behemothic belly, and the fact that he's willing to bum himself out by explaining it, lifting up his requisite black shirt and showing it anyway may offer more insight into his character than all the palm-muted power chords combined.

It began five years ago, he shares, when his balls started

hurting. This developed into a lot of unmanageable pain in the gut, and wound up being the result of a ruptured intestine. How much of the ruptured intestine was the result of his weight I do not know — it's really none of my business — although I suppose that neither is anything else I grill him about.

Anyway, it was what apparently happened next that's the story: First, his kidneys failed on the operating table, then, having survived that he was put on a Percocet diet, which he cheeked and squirreled away until he had saved up enough to get really messed up, which caused him to walk too soon and he ruptured his incision. He spent the next six months in a coma while his buddies played metal music in the hospital room; when he finally woke up, he had lost eighty pounds, or, the equivalent of an Olsen twin.

And he had a colostomy bag the size of the other one.

Now, like you, I would sooner listen to colostomy horror stories all night long than sit through a single episode of *Full House*, but after hearing himself describe watching sea snails he ate passing whole into the bag, it all became too much even for Rudy, and he suddenly tore his black shirt off in order to cap the tale and be done with it.

Rudy's ravaged belly is pretty much beyond the powers of my paltry prose. But if you must, imagine yourself wedged between Scylla and Charybdis which are themselves wedged between Grendel and Mrs. Grendel and peering into the fetid Well of Democritus, confronting a bloated patchwork of blubbery flesh ravaged by such criss-crossed hacks and cloven protoplasm as were unseen even in worst-case Rwanda — beef and brawn, adipose and collagen, sweat glands and hair follicles all drawn by some diabolical and prodigious suction into the maelstrom of his torso...

As Walton cries out upon beholding the stitched-together Frankenstein monster: *"Never did I behold a vision so horrible... I shut my eyes involuntarily."*

As did I, as did I — although when I reopened them, Rudy had already put his shirt back on, cracked a Coors Light, lit a Wildhorse, picked up the Rhoads and was laying into some gnarly licks.

By Tooth & Nail:
Mike Gill

If you have a cavity between your wisdom teeth, call a dentist. If you're feeling an increase in shoulder pain, call the *braceros*. Or, save a nickel and call Mike Gill—he can rap with authority on both.

The winery owner, a D.D.S. by degree, is now into his twelfth vintage. He claims that his rotator cuff lets him know when a pre-harvest rain is imminent—an aching arthritic phenomenon involving the effect of barometric pressure on inflammatory mediators around a joint—and plenty of studies have proven out that when folks like Mike tell you that the weather is going to change, the pain in their shoulder is not in their head.

Gill took a circuitous route to the stone-strewn hills and calcareous climbs of western Paso, and the trip that ends with Rhône-toned hits began with rinses and spits. In fact, Mike still operates the Bakersfield dental clinic where he has piloted some of the same patients from premolars to dentures. He gets top ratings, too, and is one of the more venerable fixtures in the dusty Southern California oil town, which is why he's willing to make the two hour commute from Paso Robles to Bakersfield three times a week.

Although Kern County born and bred, Gill admits that wine was never big on the family sideboard. His hometown of Taft, thirty miles southwest of Bakersfield in San Joaquin Valley's horseshoe, is among the last towns in the United States that exists primarily because of its oil reserves.
And though Kern County's agricultural output is prodigious, with grapes being a primary commodity, it also contains 81%

of California's oil wells. So if you are not in the wine biz, chances are you are an oilman, and Gills speaks with grim fondness about the local chug of choice: 'Bakersfield beer and bourbon.'

"It was a small town childhood, definitely," says Mike, seated comfortably in his museum-quality tasting room on Peachy Canyon Road. "You spent most of it making sure you did not dilute the family name. In Taft, you do what you say you're going to do; your handshake is your bond."

Funny that Mike should mention his handshake, because he has a memorable one — one of those Vise-Grip, Curly's-head-in-the-pants-press handshakes that has you down on one knee while you're publically saying hello and privately praying there's no metacarpal damage.

So, his handshake may be his bond, but it is also a pretty solid indication that with Mike Gill, you are dealing with a no-nonsense sort of up-from-the-petroleum-fields dude that does not suffer fools gladly; and because he's also exudes the aura of someone you somehow don't want to think you're a fool, much less a candy-ass fool, you grip his paw back the best you can.

Mike Gills is also the sort of fellow who manifests an overwhelming sense of focus, and this is not the kind of mindset that generally develops late in life; so, it comes as something of a surprise that he didn't hitch his wagon to two of his primary pursuits until rather late in life — although it's par for the course that he has wound up excelling at both.

More on the second avocation in a flash, but the first, of course, is wine.

Chock up Mike Gill's love of wine to serendipity. In dental

school, he had a lab partner named Geoff De Gennaro who was a food and wine person — decades ahead of his time, according to Mike. He was always inviting Mike to his house for dinner, but somehow, the stars never aligned in the precise way that made it happen. But on Easter break in 1975, Mike — who by his own admission *never* reads a Food Section — happened upon an feature in the L.A. Times called *'Bunsen Burner To Back Burner'* which wound up being about De Gennaro's passion for the culinary good life, and so impressed was Gill with the article about his old pal that he showed up to the next dinner invite with bells on.

And left with enological balls on. That night, Geoff unveiled the world of fine wine to Michael Gill, and in ways it was like when Dorothy opens the farmhouse door after landing in Oz — only, there was no tornado required, because Gill had been in the land of wine wizardry the whole time: California. Two years later, he picked up a parcel of hilly, oak-studded countryside on the west side of Paso Robles (*El Paso de Robles* is Spanish for 'Pass of the Oaks'); twenty-two acres that he describes as 'pretty barren but for the trees', neither knowing — nor then, caring — that beneath that calcareous, rock-and-acorn strewn terrain lay magical soils capable of siding with sunshine and incoming ocean air to produce wines jammed with individuality and potency: The grail of grape groupies everywhere.

Originally, even the farm advisors were gob smacked. Back in the 60's, an Orange County doctor named Stanley Hoffman had consulted with this venerable board of clodhoppers about the potential of world-class vinifera in his Paso estate, and was pretty much told to forget it. The area, he was told, was too dry, too desolate and probably too hot to grow anything of merit for the wine cellar unless that's where you stored your almonds.
But Hoffman was the sort of man to whom such a knell was a challenge, not a capital sentence, and he went on to do some

amazing things in Paso Robles, especially under the consultancy of the great André Tchelistcheff—arguably America's most influential winemaker. Hoffman had a house built for Tchelistcheff on his property and was instrumental in introducing cabernet sauvignon to the appellation.

This was a bandwagon that Mike Gill failed to climb aboard until twenty years after he'd purchased the land, an era of high inflation during which he might have done better financially by picking up a string of houses in Santa Monica. But return on investment is not the only driving force—or even a dominant one—in the hearts of most wine people— especially those like Gill who don't want to quit the day job— and when his winemaking neighbor Robert Nadeau poured him a glass of just-bottled, homegrown syrah, the lights began flashing and he suddenly envisioned a whole new dimension for his future.

"I knew," he nods, "and knew without confirmation, that Paso Robles would be the next big California wine region."

And so, he planted. First syrah, adjacent to Adelaide's pinot noir and cabernet. His first harvest was 2001, and according to Mike, it made such a bang-up product that there were figurative fistfights over who would buy his next crop. Neighbor Nadeau, along with local heroes Augie Hug and Mat Garretson (who's now producing double rye whiskey in Utah) were the last men standing, and the wine they made from his grapes was killer.

Show awards, those marketing gems, began to come in quickly for the wines these producers made, and that was all the outside confirmation that he needed to convince him that he should first be buying up more vineyard land, and second, cutting out the middlemen and proving what his grapes could do himself.

He achieved his primary goal buy picking up acres across the road and, starting in 2008 when he truly had his 'enough is enough' epiphany, by bringing on board a friend-who-will-remain-nameless (except to say that he's a Kiwi turned Bakersfield electrician) to make his wines while he drew up blueprints for Michael Gill Cellars.

Fortunately, '08 and '09 were halcyon vintages; fruit came in very ripe and making wine with it provided no massive challenges. The first wines to boast the Michael Gill label were very well received, but he did not make enough to warrant entering them into competitions.

The following summer, 2010, he enlisted Stillman Brown's skillset as winemaker for his reds; the pair had been introduced by Gill's wife Shelley two years earlier when Brown won the Syrah Shoot-Out (evidently by a huge margin) at the annual, anticipated Hospice du Rhone competition in Paso.

Stillman's winning wine formula was in lock-step with Mike's — blustering but balanced, muscular, meaty and multiplex — and before the 2010 harvest, Stillman set the stage by making passes through the vineyard, systematically removing canopy leaves, allowing more sunlight to tickle the clusters. It's a technique through which grapes become more fully 'flavor ripe' — a term with deeper denotations than merely sugar/acid ripe.

An indicator that a viticulturist may search for is the lignification of the seeds, when summer's greenish seeds darken as the vine considers it's upcoming winter shut-down; as seeds mature, they become less bitter, and since they'll stew in the must through the week or so of primary fermentation, mature seeds are a good thing. They give the harmonies required in an outstanding wine an early break.

And in the case of 2010's bang-up harvest, they did precisely that: At the 2013 Central Coast Wine Competition, Michael Gill Cellars swept the syrah competition, winning both the gold medal and Best in Class for 2010 Tuxedo Syrah, a silver for 2010 Big Rock Syrah and bronze for 2010 Black Tie Syrah.

These wines display the contemplative depth of the grape's Paso permutation, inky and extracted, often floral on the nose with tones of loganberry and pomegranate, smoky and full throughout the palate, shored by acids and gentle tannin. The original bottles, along with the awards they earned, are on prominent display in the Michael Gill Tasting Room, kitty corner to the polar bear and the arctic wolf and a slew of other slain animals: These mounts, equally, are gold medal winning trophies.

...Thus bringing us around to the second of Mike Gill's adult-onset fixations: Big game hunting.

It began with elk. Specifically, a Kaibab elk on Santa Rosa Island off the coast of Santa Barbara, the hunting of which was part of an eradication policy to remove this non-native species from the island. Gill had recently qualified to shoot a bunch of weapons, handguns to shotguns to sniping rifles, and wanted to take it to the next level. Santa Rosa had been used as a game farm for nearly a century until it was sold to the National Park Service, which allowed private hunters access to the land until 2011.

Gill bagged his ungulate and in his words, 'was hooked'.

Since then, he has traveled the globe, taking 'Top Ten' prize animals on every continent but South America (apparently, Peruvian guinea pigs are no big deal) including ibex, yak, musk ox, a bison with a .44 (it took all six chambers to drop him — I asked), a stag from Kyrgyzstan and the largest Javan Rusa deer ever shot.

Now, I have seen a few of these creatures in the wild, snorting, rooting, rutting, sometimes charging my scrawny ass, but only because my appearance within their hallowed habitat was unwelcome and intrusive.

That's fine; the long success of our species can probably be summarized in two words: 'We intruded'.

I've hunted whitetail deer and ring-neck pheasant since I was a kid, so there's no overweening moralizing from *moi*, but I do confess that when the cock flushes and I've let fly the No. 6 buckshot or when the deer steps into heart/lung range and I've released the fifty-dollar Gold Tip arrow, in retrospect the moment has always seemed to be a crime of passion.

But equally, I have watched vast strings of zebra harems track the savannah and I have seen silvery timber wolves playing in forest clearings, and it is a marvelous, memorable intrusion.

For whatever reason, having been blessed with such visions, in neither case did I feel an urge to seek out the species' alpha male, cap it, eviscerate it and have it stuffed.

On the other hand, it's sort of pushing the bounds of logic to suggest that, in surveying an autumn vineyard drooping with fat syrah clusters, there is something intrinsically obscene about seeking out the primo bunches to crush, ferment and bottle.

I have no doubt that Mike's moral compass sees big game in much the same way.

In any case, it's fascinating fuel for the mental fireplace to be pondered, perhaps, while sitting before the real one getting filled to the gills with Swilly and Gill.

SPIDERS & SPIGOTS

There's a peculiar and nearly indescribable shade of dusty greenish-gray that shows up over and over in the rolling chaparral country between Paso Robles and the sea; if Glidden had any balls, they'd have called the color 'Poached Corpse Khaki' but they don't, so their color charts refer to it as 'Artichoke Green'. It manifests itself in native artichokes, of course, but also in outcroppings of California's State Rock, metamorphic serpentine, which (incidentally) can cause magnesium imbalance and nickel toxicity in soils, making them unsuitable for vineyards — and it is also seen in the paddles of the prickly pear cacti that are scattered across the slopes and slides. It hangs from oak trees as Spanish moss and appears in the foliage of olive trees laid out by commercial growers. It's in the leaves of wild sage and then, in Scadscale scrub that ambles down to the beach of the Pacific ocean where, most dramatically, this peculiar indigenous cast puts forth its largest panorama.

Once each day, for a while, near dusk — especially when there's fog — the sea turns translucent turquoise and then as the sunsets, becomes saturated in this sublime, unutterable hue.

Highway 41 branches off from U.S. 101 at Atascadero and scrambles west through the southernmost hiccups of the Santa Lucia range which reaches its Olympus Mons in Junipero Serra Peak about fifty miles to the north. This has been, and will likely always be cattle country, so the hills — curmudgeonly, coffee-colored carbuncles a hundred million years old — are spackled with cattle dots like grains of black rice that grow larger as you draw near.
One sign advertises the made-up bovine breed as 'Brangus'; part Angus, part Brahman. The name calls to mind one those

truck stop joints where food is cooked in a made-up style called 'broasting', and I am sure that a marbled slab of broasted Brangus is to die for.

There are a couple of penned-in alpaca farms on steep hillsides where the critters run up and down in a Supersized hamster wheel. There are century plants poking up from mailboxes, spatters of desperate-looking grape vines, and on the far side, where the ocean provides enough aerosol-borne moisture, vast and gorgeous oak forests. Most are the evergreen California live oaks for which El Paso de Robles was named, but a few have begun to turn burnt orange by mid-October.

Oh, yes. There are also spiders the size of Frisbees.

Having spent two weeks patting myself on the back for having chosen an ideal month for my Paso perusal, when all the cool stuff I came to write about — grapes, olives, walnuts, almonds — are coming into harvest, I am forced to acknowledge the old caveat, *'God doesn't give with both hands…'*

Consider that to a primal arachnophobe, a tarantula is the same thing as 4:45 at the Chicago Mercantile Exchange is to an agoraphobe.

It's bungee jumping to someone with vertigo; it's a month of Friday the 13ths to a triskaidekaphobe.

It's what the sadists in Room 101 would have put inside my cage-mask make me love Big Brother.

I speed by the first one on Peachy Canyon Road, midafternoon; it appears nonchalant, ambling lazily along the shoulder of the road. I scoff, thinking I could not have just seen what I thought I saw. Then, I see a second one crawling boldly down the median, aboriginal and awful — and undeniable in its reality.

About five years ago, I saw a spider a quarter of this size on my washing machine at 4:00 AM, and considered that my options were either to fetch my .22 from the gun chest and shoot it or wake up my sleeping teenager to kill it for me. In the end, what the hell? I figured the gunshot would have woken him up anyway.

For wimps such as I from the Great Tarantula-less North, it's the least wonderful time of year. 'Tis the season for hairy, horny male Aphonopelma spiders to break celibacy vows that may have lasted for five years or more as they huddled in underground, out-of-sight-out-of-mind burrows; now, they venture forth in search of slaggy desert damsels. All well and good, but on *my* watch? Mating season lasts for weeks, and throughout, if I have a single knight in shining armor, it isn't white: It's black with rust-colored wings. The tarantula hawk is equally active during the love fest, seeking out lusting leviathans and paralyzing them to feed their young. But never fear, arachnophiles and PETA putzels — after mating, a male tarantula lives only a few months anyway, and if the wasp strikes after that, the female spider is likely to lay a thousand eggs for future frightening love fests.

You may see these skulking succubi everywhere across vast ochre biome, but the one thing you will not see is water. It's dry — so dry that every time there is a serious thunderstorm, new religions form.

Adding insult to aridity, San Luis Obispo has been in the throes of drought for several years now, and in August, 2013, the National Drought Mitigation Center changed the county's status from D2, severe drought, to D3, extreme drought.

Rainfall for the past two years has made it the third driest period on record since 1870 — the year that weather observations started. Cal Poly, where climatic data is centered, measured only 3.5 inches of rain before the August alert kicked in. An average year would have brought nearly five times that much.

Although it doesn't take a Cal Poly degree in Critical Thinking to recognize that the responsible culprit here is the Man Upstairs with his sprinkling can, that doesn't stop locals from casting stick and stones at one another.

And a lot of the ammunition ends up in vineyards.

According to Susan Luft, president of the all-volunteer PRO Water Equity, Inc., the problem isn't rain — it's rapacity.

"Water levels are dropping throughout the majority of the Paso Robles groundwater basin, regardless of whether it's a wet or dry year. The basin cannot supply all of the demands; it is in overdraft."

Luft owns ten acres in the Creston sub-area of the Paso Robles Groundwater Basin, and since 2000, when she purchased the property, she has seen the water level in her well drop over a hundred feet. As her home is on the edge of the groundwater basin, drilling a deeper well would require penetrating Monterey Shale, with low flow rate, uncertain production and poorer water quality.

The Paso Robles Groundwater Basin encompasses 790 square miles and is the sole source of water for the majority of northern SLO County. Luft cites studies indicating that only a few years ago, the basin was at its safe yield. No longer, and she insists that agriculture is the primary beneficiary of the limited resource (67%), often to the detriment of Paso Robles urban and residential use (30%).

"Agriculture, and especially vineyards, are vital to our economy, to be sure," she says (and as the owner of a small vineyard, she should know), "but if the water goes, they're out of business anyway."

And there are few alternatives: "The only sources of supplemental water are limited, extremely expensive, and unlikely to be available for a decade or more. Reduced groundwater pumping is the only method of reducing the declines in the foreseeable future."

The counterpoint is taken up by an admirer of hers, one of Susan Luft's neighbors, winemaker Don Brady, who sees the situation from both sides — as a commercial wine grower and a residential homeowner and perhaps, with a little Texas prudence stirred in for spice:

"I see a bunch of lawyers swooping in to sue everybody, and in the end, there's no more water than there was before."

He points out that Susan's statistics may be correct, but in the wider picture, grape vines use far less irrigation water than the commodities they replaced, mostly alfalfa and sugar beets. A stressed grape is a delicious grape, so drip irrigation is held to a minimum, and plenty of vineyards are entirely dry-farmed.

"Paso agriculture uses half the water today that it did in the '70s, before the wineries came in," he maintains. "Meanwhile, the population has grown from seven thousand residents in 1970 to over thirty thousand today."

A lot of these new households rely on water from 200-foot wells, he says, and that tends to pull up the transient water.

"'Google Earth' Paso Robles," he suggests. "Look at all the swimming pools."

Brady believes that the county basin has enough water that, if used judiciously, should last another three thousand years.

"If we haven't found a way out of this by then, we probably deserve what we get."

Both Brady and Luft agree that solution is likely to be political, but so long as this public resource is not used as a political bargaining chip and neither side uses the other as a punching bag, they are okay with that. Luft is big proponent of fair and equitable allocation of groundwater for all users through proper management of the basin, and this will require the establishment of an official water district.

In the interim, eco-friendly vineyard manager are cutting waste anywhere they can, using small pumps and slowly filling up ponds on their properties during non-peak usage hours.

"Wasting water," Don points out, "is like burning C-notes."

BRADY'S BUNCHES:
ROBERT HALL WINERY

If another 6.5 magnitude earthquake hits Paso Robles like the one that collapsed the city's landmark clock tower in 2003 — and it will — you'd be challenged to find yourself in a better situation than touring the 19,000 square foot cavern under Robert Hall Winery.

The 4000 barrel cave, equipped with a series of swamp coolers for humidity and temperature control, keeping it at wine-ideal 55 - 60° F. Designed by Robert Hall himself and mined by Nick Pokrajac of nearby Templeton, the caverns — completed in 2001 — were dug using the cut and fill technique conventionally employed in hard-rock ore extraction.

The caves can accommodate 289 guests and/or earthquake refugees; it was engineered to withstand a quake of 8.5 on the Richter scale, considerably more powerful than the one that leveled San Francisco in 1906.

Robert Hall's three-hundred acre estate on Paso's east side began in concept in the 1970s when a trip to the Rhône Valley convinced the Minnesota entrepreneur and horse-breeder that the winery good life might be a better introduction to his autumn years. I will not say 'his retirement years' because if I did I might wind up like Fortunato, walled up in one of the cellar niches. Indeed, Robert Hall is hardly ready for the ice floe. He works his own vineyards tirelessly, even today, and can as often be seen shadowing the cellar rats or lording over the tasting room. And when he isn't there, he's likely globe hopping, schmoozing, promoting product — which is one of the reasons why his wines can be found in virtually every state.

Prior to breaking vineyard ground in 1995, Hall and his wife Margaret wandered California appellations to find the right soil and climate for his pet varietals from Rhône, and like a few before him and many since, discovered it in Paso Robles. That year, he purchased Home Ranch in the rolling hills above the Estrella Plain, and later, Terrace Vineyard overlooking the Estrella River, Bench Vineyard, where the estates most intense reds are grown, and the 18-acre Brady Vineyard, planted to cabernet sauvignon and cabernet franc and named for Don Brady, Robert Hall's winemaker.

More on Don in a flash.

Robert Hall's goal for the winery's production was around 100,000 cases—a target that he has not yet hit, although producing wine for other wineries with the additional capacity is a good way to keep the crew busy and cover the cost of goods. Half of Hall's acres are planted to cabernet sauvignon, but he's planted thirteen of his beloved 'Rhône' varietals and five traditional grapes of Oporto, which are blended to make Robert Hall Vintage Port; 2009 is the current release.

In the on-site laboratory, one Hall hallmarks is here marked: Frequent focus is placed upon color monitoring and quantifiable tannin measurement; both play as vital a role in vinification decisions as sugar and acid levels. Color, of course, is vital in evaluating Rhônes in Rhône; reds must display deep and characteristic ruby tones when young and if the bricky orange rim kicks in before the wine is seven or eight years old, something is amiss.

And Don Brady knows it. It's down to his technical background, reaped and honed in the laboratories and llanos of Texas, where he learned his craft.

Brady was born in Navasota, Texas—a small town in a small

world since it's also where my buddy Bridget hails from—and he picked up his horticultural degree from Texas Tech. As a budding winemaker, he could not have picked a better time or place in which to study. The University of Texas owns over a million acres of land in the western half of the state and they have never quite figured out what to do with it beyond oil leasing. They've tried fruit orchards, they've tried eucalyptus groves, and with some of the run-off cash from the oil, they've tried grape vines.

And Don, at Texas Tech, found himself as a benefactor of some of the shared wealth.

At this time, as in many states following Prohibition, the Texas wine industry was finally in the process of re-inventing itself. It's an interesting history, for sure, and I'm sure that even most Texans would be surprised to learn that their state has more native Vitis grape vine species than any other region on earth and that Franciscans were making wine near El Paso a hundred years before California missionaries planted their first vine. Small wonder that Brady's agricultural department was chomping at the bit to establish data and figure out why their gigantic, ideally situated high desert was not producing more quality wine—less, in fact, than even miniscule Sancerre.

Brady reminisces about his college days, working the vineyards by day and running sample tests in a basement chemistry lab by night. That sort of fast-paced, candle-at-both-ends learning curve saw him pick up a lot of information quickly and led him to his first industry job at Llano Estacado winery, which he helped steer from a 13,000 case winery to a production of more than 80,000 cases annually.

Brady was in on a similar ground-floor growth explosion at his next post at Ste. Genevieve Wines in Bakersfield, Texas. This was near his family's home in Fort Stockton, and he says wistfully, "I always wanted to return to my roots, and to my great chagrin, I got my wish."

It was not necessarily his wife fondest wish, however: Kasi Brady had grown up there too and insisted that after having spent twenty years trying to get out of west Texas, she was not eager to spend the rest of Don's working life there. So, even after having been awarded the Texas Wine and Grape Growers Association's highest honor, the '1991 Louis F. Qualia Award' for outstanding contributions and leadership in the Texas wine, by 1999 he sensed that it was time to shift gears and move west to the epicenter of the American wine industry in California.

And two years later, that's exactly where Robert Hall found him, as senior winemaker at Delicato Family Vineyards, bouncing back and forth between Modesto and King City. By that point, Don was getting a bit weary of long commutes and producing wine in big box bulk — even good stuff.

A single walk through the vineyards with Robert convinced both of them that they'd seen the future, and it was now, and not only that, it was going to be (as the Texans say) walkin' in tall cotton.

"I wanted to grow with a vertically-integrated winery," Don nods. "...the appellation, the vineyards and people with the will and ability to develop signature, house-styles; the best wines that Paso Robles could produce."

He found his vintner's Valhalla, his lone star, among the alluvial soils and uplifted seabed of several of Paso Robles' 'bubbles' — areas where climatic influence from the Pacific and soil composition, whose value may be determined by mountain run-off and the kaleidoscopic arrangement of solids and pores — a world away from the plains of Texas, where the vagaries of nature can wipe out a crop in a single day and quarter of the counties still have dry laws on the books.

These days, Brady's sugar-poppin' palate-pleasers may be more Beach Boys than Lyle Lovett, less 'Texas T' black gold and more Forty-Niner nugget gold, but his colloquialisms damn sho' ain't, and listening to his gentle, lilting Abilene drawl is half the fun in chatting with him. His 'fine wine' become his *'fahhn wahhn'*, choosing a vineyard site becomes *'fahhndin' the rahht abode'* and when his corkscrew doesn't work, it's *'womperjawed'*.

Which detracts nothing from the technical alchemy in his constant data mining in the winery lab and profound understanding of the art of his gig — wine's journey from root to Riedel.

I would not hesitate to say that Don Brady is among the sharpest tools in the wine science shed that I have encountered anywhere in the United — *straahk* that — the *'YOO-nahted States'*.

And in terms of bringing in the bling, Brady has also proved his medal mettle. Personally, his acclaim includes being the 2001 recipient of the International Wine and Spirits Competition 'Wine of America' award, and he was recognized by the Paso Robles Wine Country Alliance (in partnership with the Independent Grape Growers of Paso Robles and San Luis Obispo Vintners Association) as Winemaker of the Year in 2006.

His wares have done as swimmingly, but reached truly remarkable heights in 2010 at the State Commercial Wine Competition, which considers itself the oldest and most prestigiously judged wine competition in North America.

Faced with a pool of more than six hundred competing wineries and three thousand entries, Robert Hall Winery took home so many individual awards--Five Best of Class (South

Central Coast Appellation) honors, three gold and seven silver medals — that it was named 'Golden State Winery, 2010', the first time that in the competition's history that a Paso Robles winery, or even a winery from the greater Central Coast AVA, had been so honored.

And like that dude who was so impressed with his Remington shaver that he bought the company, Don Brady was so wowed by his new digs that he bought the farm: Eighteen acres of prime cabernet country on a sweet spot on the first bench above the Estrella river, where the soils are sandy and open.

Besides his cabernet sauvignon, which he maintains is Paso Robles' destiny grape both as a commercial cash cow and horticultural gem ("It reflects Paso Robles and amounts to more than half of what do here"), he is hugely high on petite sirah, for which his land seems ideally suited. He admits that petite sirah can be a hand-sell among those who confuse it with Robert Hall Winery's other primo cultivar, syrah, but once sampled, Brady's is hard to forget. Blackstrap black, both bright and brooding, Brady has overcome two of the grape's failings in other single-varietal versions: He's tamed the tannins and avoided an overt prunishness that comes from grapes picked too ripe.

Fair to say, there is nothing petite about Brady's petite sirah beyond the name.

'Hammer of the Gods' is a descriptor used by Stillman Brown to describe a truly remarkable wine, and it can mean anything from in-your-face to over-the-top. Don Brady's concoctions may be, on occasion, a little of the first but are rarely the second.

He believes that his primary objective is 'to not screw anything up'. His wines whisper loudly; his winemaking philosophy is a 'quest for the good; an extension of the stewardship that begins in the vineyard.'

As a result, there is appealing, if indefinable elegance to Don's wine—a transcendent sense of balance among the myriad minutes and infinite incidentals that go into a superb glass of wine.

There's grace to his grape, and I think it's down to an intangible Texas touch.

Ab Fab:
The Abalone Farm

Busting the myth that you can't hurry art, Chateau d'Abalone 2013 hit the market so quickly that you had to wonder if Stillman Brown imported the grapes from Australia, where the growing season is six month ahead of ours. But no, the fruit is pure Paso, picked in early September of this year.

Touchstones are important things in small town reality, and Stillman is eager to show me the very kitchen table where he first conceived the wonderful wine and atrocious pun he calls Chateau d'Abalone — a beverage designed specifically to pair with Cayucos' most highbrow export, abalone.

The table is the kitchen centerpiece in the kempt but sea-weathered, shanty-esque home shared by Brad Buckley and Mike Shecora on a craggy vista overlooking Morro Bay. Alas, the table is ordinary and fails to capture me with its historical significance.

But the plates of abalone sure do. Four different preparations by Brad, each one simpler than the one before, showcase the sanctity of simplicity when preparing this buttery, delicate mollusk.

Abalone has been a coastal food source for twelve thousand years, although not likely as a result of the encyclopedia's description: 'A gastropod related to the sea slug, also called muttonfish, from the genus haliotis' — which is unrelated to bad breath; I checked.

But, talk about ugly? If ever the rubric 'you can't judge a book by its cover' has a poster child, it's abalone, particularly the red abalone, which looks like a dirty brick wrapped in a Brillo pad.

Ah, but pop that shell and you will find out what a hundred twenty-five dollars per pound can buy you: Pure, sweet, ethereal flesh nestling within a shell so iridescent that it's used to ornament altars and as inlay for musical instruments.

Or disco balls. Before he even shows me the kitchen table, Brad takes me to his tiny, obsessively-organized clutter of a workshop in the back of his house and proudly unveils his latest nacre sculpture — a full-sized, ready-for-2001-Odyssey-on-a-feverish-Saturday-night glitter ball hand made from abalone shells.

The ball nestles alongside another work of art — a shell-studded horse skull — that hangs near a solid wall of mother-of-pearl; two thousand individual abalone shells forming a vertical panorama.

I'm not sure if you can become an abaloneophile like you can become a Francophile or a bibliophile, but if you can, Brad Buckley is one. Initially, he began picking up occasional cash-paying grunt work here at the 18 acre farm, intending to make some pocket money while he looked for a 'real job' in public administration: A quarter century later, he's still here.

He has risen through the ranks of course, and now manages the place; along the way has learned so much about the delicate art of tank-raising mollusks that after he's done with the tour, you feel like you've lived a second life as an abalone farmer.

From a distance, the rows of concrete tanks, decaying to rebar, smelling of fish and brine and perched on a crumbling cliff above the ocean, look very third world. Once in among the nuts and bolts of the operation, however, things perk up immediately.

Or rather, percolate up. The flow of the farm begins in the large, covered breeding tanks where wild abalone (now protected and caught only with a special license) are used as brood stock; they broadcast spawn, which means that fertilization occurs in the water, outside the bodies of ma and pa.

It's a quick path to babyhood — eggs hatch within twenty-four hours and look like poppy seeds sprinkled throughout the tank. That changes as they begin their lifetime mission of seaweed munching; in the nascent stage, the hatchlings consume so much chlorophyll-colored algae that they soon turn green themselves, turning the tank into verdant slurry.

After a few months, the abalone have grown into toddlers — fingernail-sized and able to cling to the side of the tank and move about, but not climb over the edge. Strips of AstroTurf ringing the tank ensure that the brave and the few don't decide they're proud enough to storm any emplacements.

At ten months, they move outdoors to concrete tanks filled with moving seawater, replicating the intertidal zone in which they'd survive naturally.

And you can see these pools, turquoise and shimmering with sunlight, in the near distance.

A hundred years ago, abalone were so numerous along this coast that they could be plucked from rocks at low tide. And they were: Abalone fishing reached peaks in the 1950s and '60's, and so ferociously were the predators that California

Fish and Game Commission ended commercial fishing for wild abalone in 1997, although other factors — including disease, global warming (increasing carbon dioxide in sea water, effectively raising pH beyond what they can tolerate) and the proliferation of sea otters, who can eat their weight in abalone in an afternoon — added to the decline

And in fairness, some of the blame must go to the mollusk itself for being such a damn slowpoke.

A grape vine may take three years before it produces any useable wine fruit, but an abalone requires four to six years to reach marketable size in this environment: Around four ounces of live weight. The slowness of their maturation is undoubtedly a limiting factor in the establishment of more abalone farms: Patience may be a virtue, but paying the mortgage is an imperative.

At least, for the per-pound price they command, abalone are cheap dates, low-maintenance easy, and Purina has not yet seen a market for Mollusk Chow. Abalone eat kelp and only kelp, and that is readily harvested from the bay.

And it's sustainable, too — kelp regenerates itself at a rate that is the diametrical opposite of abalone's snail pace growth and can extend its length by as much as three feet a day.

As such, it completes the cycle of what is perhaps the most eco-friendly form of aquaculture in current practice.

Hard to say who farms the best abalone in the California, but if it becomes a contest, The Abalone Farm will be in the top ten.

Before anyone starts printing t-shirts, consider that there are only eight commercially licensed abalone farms to begin with.

The aptly named Abalone Farm is the largest, oldest and most bare-bones-looking mollusk farm in the United States, housing as many as six million abalone at any given time and accounting for nearly half of all the homegrown abalone sold — they market more than a quarter million pounds per year, either as tenderized steaks — pre-pounded and shrink-wrapped — or live in the shell. (Live in-the-shell abalone about a third of its weight in steaks).

If you happen to be a fan of scallops fan in their butter-sweet and briny glory, you'll find the flavor of abalone equally user-friendly — as easy on the palate as it is tough on the pocket book.

True bay scallops — the best and costliest of the scallop breed — are mostly trapped on the East Coast during the winter, but abalone is a year-round phenomenon. Preparation philosophy is the same: Fresher is better and less is more; err on the side of undercooking and don't go all baroque on the saucing.

In fact, of the three recipes that Brad whips up in his boathouse kitchen, the most exotic ingredient he uses is bread crumbs.

Tenderizing a raw abalone flesh — actually, a 'foot' of muscle that allows the snail its locomotion — requires some elbow grease.

Brad separates the meat from the shell with a self-sharpened spoon, running in along the concave inner surface — the iridescent side — until the piece yields.

At this point, Brad having snipped off the strand of viscera and removed the bitter black film, abalone is, to connoisseurs, at its peak of perfection — wonderfully flavorful when sliced paper-thin, salty, sweet — and crunchy tough.

The texture of raw abalone is an acquired preference to be sure; it's a bit like biting into a rubber band. To win over newbie scallop people, the meat has to be relaxed, which is done by pounding the slices with a meat mallet for a few moments. Brad places his on a cutting board between strips of plastic wrap, which prevents splatter and keeps the meat intact.

It takes a minute or so, but the resulting slices are foie-gras tender.

Crudo (raw) and sashimi-dressed may be best, but if you prefer it cooked, quickly sautéed in butter yields phenomenal results. Dusted with bread crumbs and fresh herbs adds an unnecessary, but still scrumptious variation on a theme.

I won't argue the need for wine as the proper abalone accompaniment, because that is as horse and carriagey as love and marriage in the old Sinatra tune.

For shellfish in general, lightly cooked or raw, unadorned white wine with intense, clean flavors tend to work better than oaked wine that has had time to think about it and maybe taken on a bit of oxidation. Half-shell oysters and Muscadet, prawns and sémillon, Chablis with mussels are classic matches; Abalone farm abalone and Stillman Brown's Chateau d'Abalone 3013 may wedge its way into the pantheon.

First, the grape:

Up until the 1980s, verdejo was nearly forgotten even in its native Rueda; it is one of those indigenous varietals that may owe its survival to a single source, in this case Marqués de Riscal. Along with Émile Peynaud — the Frenchman whose classic treatise *Knowing and Making Wine* helped Stillman Brown to cut his winemaking chops — the revered house in northern Spain began to vinify verdejo into a light, lively wine intended to be consumed within a year or two. Any longer, and the wine develops the nutty quality prized in Sherry (also made in part, pre-phylloxera, with verdejo), but somewhat off-putting in a youthful white.

Taking a cue from the cream-sweet flesh of the abalone, Stillman has fashioned a dry wine that skitters between herb and fruit; it shows a grassy pineapple charm that, owing to the grapes high acidity and glycerol, has a remarkably luscious — almost viscous — mouthfeel.

The grapes in Chateau d'Abalone 2013 were picked in late August and released in bottled form five weeks later, an almost unheard-of turnaround time. But it works; Stillman was looking to avoid what he refers to as 'turbidity' — a word often used in connection with oak-aged reds and referring to a certain cloudiness in wine that may be considered a flaw.

The wine has a slight hint of sulphur, which blows off quickly, and in the end, Chateau d'Abalone settles alongside Brad Buckley's sublime abalone with absolute authority.

And that's no baloney.

THE ALPHA BOAR: GARY EBERLE

The downside of owning an Irish Setter, Gary Eberle recalls with exuberance, is that they shed more than an oak tree after a frost.

But, that's also the upside: It's safer to get some strange, so long as she's a redhead.

That is, of course, no longer a consideration for the native of Coraopolis — a tiny steel town near Pittsburgh — who is now happily ensconced in the vice-grip sanctity of a second marriage. He's now poodle-whipped, which is to say that as a dog owner he's switched to poodles, though not the ankle-biting toys that Zsa Zsa likes: The big, black, lion-cut kind.

And, in the fashion of big, jovial, brash men everywhere who do big things in a big way, Eberle's poodles are treated like celebrities. They greet tasting room guests with barks or tail wags depending on their mood, and today, they lounge lazily beneath an outside bedizened with plaques that commemorate those Eberle poodles who have gone before them.

Each had a grape name: Chardonnay, Syrah, Cabernet (Zinfandel and Rousanne are still alive), and each memorial has a brief description of the dog's personality — evidence of Gary Eberle's careful attention to nuance and detail.

Of himself he says, "When I go, my plaque will be up there for sure. It's gonna say, 'He was the Alpha Male'."

No argument here. First, Gary is not just gigantic, he's

football gigantic, and he's not just football gigantic but defensive tackle football gigantic, which is exactly the position he played for Penn State's Nittany Lions in the 1960s.

It's also fitting that he has a black cat named Mephistopheles, which Stillman Brown, ever lost in Elvismania, refers to as 'Memphistopheles'. Fitting because in Goethe's *Faust,* Mephistopheles first appears in the form of a black poodle — an irony that may or may not be lost on the Eberle clan.

Anyway, about his strange and spectacular career, Eberle maintains, "I've had two heroes in my life: Robert Mondavi and Joe Paterno."

It's not tough to see why. These were strong, über-masculine men known for integrity of purpose and a tough-love approach to mentoring young folks in whom they recognized the tug of potential, and both saw it in Eberle.

"Any success I've had so far in life I owe to them far more than to myself," he admits with candor and constraint.

Among a host of lessons that Mondavi taught him, Eberle shares, is the omnipotence of marketing: "He'd tell me that in California, anyone can make decent wine. The trick is selling it for what it's worth, and to as wide an audience as possible. His genius was seeing, believing, promoting. Alone, Robert Mondavi never made a bottle of wine in his life, and he was the first one to acknowledge it."

And the statement is pretty much true — part of a universal dichotomy: A winemaker is not necessarily a person who makes wine. Mondavi founded a number of philosophical schools that transformed the industry — first and foremost, that California did not have to ride in the wine jalopy's rumble seat while French people drove.

He understood that the West Coast in general, and Napa in particular, was capable of producing product that could rival the greatest wines of Europe.

Throughout his life, Mondavi traveled extensively and networked with numerous numens; in many ways, his partnership with Baron Philippe de Rothschild of Bordeaux's Château Mouton-Rothschild (creating Opus One) legitimized his mission in the eyes of many skeptics, especially those with pockets deep enough to invest. At the coinciding inaugural Napa Valley Wine Auction of 1981, a single case of the debut vintage of Opus One sold for a stratospheric $24,000.

And, of course, even so, Opus One wound up being as much a symbol as a label, since many bottle sharks feel that the wine itself never quite lived up to the hype, especially as the synthesis of two of the world's greatest wine minds.

Another representative notch in Mondavi's legacy belt is Fumé Blanc, a clever costume in which to disguise sauvignon blanc, which he had previously vinified as somewhat flabby and sweet. Derived in name and style from dry, flinty, often oak-fermented sauvignon blancs from the Loire Valley's Pouilly-Fumé, the acute directional turn single-handedly brought this varietal to national notice and popularity.

And, perhaps exemplifying Mondavi's go-team-go California cheerleading, he did not patent the name, but permitted any winery to call their sauvignon blanc Fumé Blanc, so long as it was dry.

Oddly, both Opus One and Fumé Blanc are exceptions that prove Mondavi's rule: California is far better off labeling wines under a varietal name than a place name, or worse, under a fawning, faux-French small-letter rip-off like 'chablis' or 'burgundy' or the *ne plus nadir*, 'sauterne' which the semi-genericists couldn't even spell right. Having measured top

Côte-d'Or reds against Burgundy's worst stewy plonk in an attempt the extract the alchemic differences, Mondavi produced what was, at the time, California's best pinot noir.

These days, in Paso Robles, the cavalcade of single-variety wines has grown exponentially because, unlike climate-fickle France, where certain grapes grow in certain pockets and that's that, in California, with managed irrigation and judicious plot-picking, you can grown just about anything just about anywhere.

Gary Eberle laments, "All I ever wanted to do was to make cabernet sauvignon! I wanted to be Joe Heitz. Now I grow twenty different varieties — it's obscene!"

Still, cab remains king at Eberle Winery, and it may be as much about nostalgia as it is about druthers. Gary reminisces about the path that led him to the painted plywood planks of Pennsylvania, where he was raised by a single parent (his mother, whom he grimly refers to as 'a truly frightening woman; a sociopath' — his earliest memory is being beaten with a high-heeled shoe and being stuck in the leg with a dinner fork) to the potentate of the Central Coast Wine Competition 's 2013 'Winery of the Year'; Eberle's Bordeaux-blends have been instrumental in the estate becoming the single most awarded winery in the country.

Sort of strange to think it began with a bottle of Mateus. But back in the day, among wine people wannabes, this strange pink Portuguese rosé, a few bucks per ping-pong-paddle-shaped bottle, was *comme il faut* (along with Lancer's and Blue Nun) at dinner parties, at least the kind that Eberle was used to.

For whatever reason, Eberle had by that point developed a

non-gridiron interest in classical opera, and the sort of dinner parties that featured soundtracks by Berlioz and Verdi tended to feature brighter wine stars. He was introduced to Lynch Bages, Latour and Montrachet, and with his competitive nature in full bloom, conceded honest defeat while relegating future bottles of Mateus to the purpose for which they are better suited: Candle holders.

By that time, he'd graduated from Penn State with a degree in Zoology — a counselor had pushed him that direction — and gone on to LSU, where the field of genetic research was coming on board in a big way.

In those callow days of safe decisions, Eberle's aim was to become a teacher (college level, where he figured that his libido might be of less concern to law enforcement than high school), but even on a fast track to a Ph. D, the more he drank wine, the more Eberle came to the unsettling conclusion that'd he'd rather be a alcoholic than a co-ed-scamming, pencil-shoving geneticist.

And that's exactly what he told Professor Berg at the University of California Davis — or words to that effect.

Created by the California Legislature in 1880, U.C. Davis' Department of Viticulture and Enology is to wannabe winemakers what M.I.T. is to fledgling rocket scientists. Appointed to the Chair in 1967, the same year that Amerine and Joslyn published *Table Wines; The Technology of Their Production in California*, Harold (Hod) Berg was noted for brevity and succinctness, and accepted Eberle into a doctoral program without an exam.

And so, Eberle completed the coast-hopping that had begun in steel country, arriving in Davis, California with $600 in cash and a vintage Bonneville, where he began to forge a legacy which has made him (according to *IntoWine*) among the top 100 most influential winemakers in the world, calling him, 'The Godfather of Paso Robles'.

But why Paso Robles, the eno hinterland, when a fellow with a cabernet complex might have easily have landed in civilized North Country? Napa or Sonoma? Especially because, although the Franciscan Friars had first planted grapes in the Paso region in the eighteenth century, nobody had really taken advantage of the place since the Prohibition, not even grape growers, who thought the heat and fractured soils better suited to zinfandel?

Because the professors at Davis knew better.

Having tagged along with Dr. Harold Olmo on soil analysis field trips (in the role of Sherpa packhorse, digging and bagging samples), he gradually became as infatuated with Paso's potential as his teachers, who shook their heads at the oversight of all but three California winemakers; at that time, the others were opting to establish wineries in trendier sites up north.

Eberle declares that he was drawn to take the lead of role models like Joe Heitz and Georges de Latour and put down roots in Napa, but Professor Olmo talked him out of it:

"Didn't we teach you *anything* at Davis? This is the ground you want: The poorest soils make the best wine."

In the end, it was indeed a dirt thing, and the plot of land Eberle ended up with was one that late Dr. Olmo — then one of the world's most revered viticulturists — was very high on. Calcareous slate and shale, more sand than limestone (says Eberle, "There's not enough limestone in Paso Robles to make a bag of cement"), and unlike many available sites, where cross-type soils would make obligatory irrigation difficult as different soil soaks up water at different rates, this one boasted a single subterranean structure.

It was on the east side of Paso Robles, where it is very dry and without much natural vegetation, tending to make soils loamy and better capable of water retention. If you're growing artichokes, fertile ground is a good thing. If you're making estate cabernet, it's not.

And it was cheap: The land, which was highway deeded so you could enter it directly from Route 46 without having to bug your neighbors for an access road, could be had for $200 per acre, and it was of a type which could not be had today for $50,000 per.

But for a dude with a beat-up Bonneville, either sum was a pipe dream, and that meant investors. Luckily, his half-brothers were looking to expand, and for the first time, Gary Eberle had to strap on his Mondavi-inspired salesman's chainmail and convince them that this was the hinterland hot spot that would make them all a fortune.

They nibbled the bait, and together, the Eberle brothers bought seven hundred acres on which Gary planted cabernet sauvignon, syrah, zinfandel, barbera, sauvignon blanc and chenin blanc.

The whites were a mistake, Gary now owns: "The sauvignon blanc was out of control; the leaves were the size of dinner plates and the fruit was abundant, but sort of soap-flavored. As for chenin blanc, it needs too much water. The only way you should grow that stuff out here is hydroponically."

He made 8,000 cases that first year and sold it all with a hiccup, and all concerned were convinced that they had tapped the moolah motherload. They began to steadily up the quantities produced until they maxed at 300,000 cases in

1981. That was during the California wine boom, of course, when unsustainable heights were hit. Sales slowed, but it was just as well — this was not the kind of bulk production that Eberle was interested in anyway.

The following year, he approached his partners with a proposal: He'd take his shares in sweat equity and wine at $18 per case and re-establish the label as a small production winery specializing in two wines, cabernet and chardonnay.

Which is precisely what he did, although Eberle admits to having tossed in a third wine, a Krug-knockoff, high sugar, low-alcohol muscat: "The only formula wine I have ever made."

In its current incarnation, Eberle Winery started out producing less than 20,000 cases annually, creeping up 25,000 and will, in 2014, do a two-step slide up to 30,000 cases, which Gary believes will be the company's final build-up.

As a winemaker, though, he insists that he reached his productive peak a dozen years ago, and so, in 2003, enlisted as his winemaker the brilliant Ben Mayo, an employee who had begun his Eberle career as a cellar worker.

Mayo brings both art and science to the program, having earned a degree in cultural anthropology from UC Santa Cruz and having done a six-year stint at Francisco's famed John Bergguren Gallery, where he honed knowledge of highbrow art along with highbrow wine. He considers that his science left-brain helps before harvest and that when it comes to creating elegant blends and isolating 'Eberle-defining' subtleties in raw juice, his artistic right-brain side kicks in.

It's easy to see that a prize-peppered show-stopper like his 2007 Reserve Estate Cabernet Sauvignon — winner of a gold medal/Best of Class at the Pacific Rim Wine Competition,

2012; a gold medal at the Sommelier Challenge, 2011; a gold medal at the San Diego International Wine Competition, 2012; gold medal at the Consumer Wine Awards at Lodi, 2012, etc. — is indeed a steady, slow-drip irrigation of brain juice from both hemispheres.

That said, 2007 truly was a wonder year in Paso, a classic vintage that began with a cold and dry winter and led to a low-rainfall (40% less than average) growing season that stressed the vines and showcased low yields of concentrated fruit with natural tannins that wound up being more mellow than the intensity of the grapes might have campaigned for.

Overall, Gary Eberle is not an advocate of the theory that lower yields equal better wine, and he has a cellar's worth of wine to prove him out, but even he points out that if you made a crappy cabernet in 2007 you should consider buying a gas station.

Still, there are a whole lot more gas station owners in California than gifted winemakers, and Eberle has taken Ben Mayo into his family, making him a partner and coaching him the way that he was coached by JoePa at a time where he only aim in life was 'to play football and get laid.'

Nearly two years after Joe Paterno's death and half a century after his college career, Gary Eberle still gets choked up when discussing the path to conscience and classiness to which the Brooklyn-born coach steered him. Paterno, of course, saw many of his wins stripped away by a hasty—and many believe precipitous and unjust—sanction by the NCAA in the wake of the Jerry Sandusky child sex abuse scandal of 2012. In fact, so absurd does the whole situation seem in hindsight—blaming Paterno, who seems to have followed protocol in reporting the report he'd been given by an assistant coach to Athletic Director Tim Curley and Gary Schultz, who oversaw the University Police—that Eberle's tears quickly turn to fatalistic anger and black humor:

"Yeah," he says, "you should probably blame me more than Paterno. I played with Jerry Sandusky [a Penn State defensive end, 1963 – 1965] and crouching down in front of him in my tight polyester must have driven him over to the dark side…"

Of course, such nonsense quickly returns to the realm of the real, especially when he describes his visit to Joe's widow Sue [Suzanne Pohland, whom he married in 1962 when she was a Penn State English literature honors student and he, assistant coach] last year: "I brought her an imperial of cabernet with '409' etched on the back in commemoration of Joe's 409 victories as head coach.'

Actually, if you count Gary Eberle among Paterno's wins, that number might better be listed as 410.

Such a Pennsylvania homecoming must be somewhat bittersweet for Eberle, who lost as much a father figure as a friend when Joe Paterno passed away in January, 2012. This conclusion seems inescapable when you consider that Gary, by his own admission, spent less than 48 hours in total with his own father, although the taciturn mill worker only lived a couple miles away.

It was the fallout of the era, it was the tradition, and it was, apparently, the wish of Gary's mother, who was as strong-willed as she was strong-armed: When he was ten years old, she cold-cocked him, knocked him silly and administered the only non-football-related concussion he'd ever suffered.

But he points out that his name (and logo icon) means 'young boar' in *Sprachraum*, also known as 'farmer's German'.

And boars, of course, are known for several interesting traits: They tend to be somewhat solitary outside of breeding season, and when cornered, become nearly unstoppably aggressive, charging without regard for self, and nearly always coming out ahead of the game in any fray.

And that's a good enough metaphor for Gary Eberle's raucous ride to the top, bootstraps to boutique blends, steel town to style town.

¡ Viva Vermentino !

The sun is creeping upward, angling through the chilly valley fog, just clearing the oak groves on the far horizon and illuminating the uppermost leaves along the vine rows.

That sun, soft enough at dawn, will soon become a blazing saboteur. Off will come the hoodies and parkas. The field workers are all small and dark-skinned, earnest and coffee-fueled. And I'm late. By the time I pick my first grape, their gloved hands are already shiny with a patina of sticky vermentino juice and they have half a ton in the bin.

As the day warms, an advance guard of yellow jackets moves in — a bane of the seasonal workforce. Every once in a while, you'll encounter grapes that have been plundered by these wasps, hollow shells of skin, blackened and useless.

The workers are resilient, stumping through the rows, one hand on a bunch, the other snipping the so-called peduncle. There's a degree of experience required, and these men have it — wasp grapes, moldy grapes, unripe grapes are not wanted in the bins, which will not be sorted before crushing.

As I alluded to earlier, on the last part of my train ride into town, Los Angeles to Paso on the Coast Starlight, I sat with a leathery old Mexican migrant worker from Guadalajara.

His English was stilted and my Spanish was worse, but having spent time in tequila country, he and I found some common ground.

His name was Emiliano, and our Paso purpose was linked; he was picking up seasonal work in the same vineyards I was writing about.

Like those fascinating old stories from hobos on *Tales From The Rails* who learned the rules of the road and the cultural etiquette of transient camps, I tapped him for some taste of the life of a *trabajador agrícola migrante*, of which, in any given year, the United States may host five million.

And by 'life', I could not find a more apt lexeme.

Emiliano began his career (he sees it as such; not a 'job') as a *bracero* half a century ago, picking strawberries at an age when most American kids are still picking noses. At eight, working in hellish heat, he was paid the equivalent of ten dollars for six twelve-hour days hunching at a 90-degree angle and stuffing berries into a gawky one-wheeled cart. All field work is hard, but nearly all migrants agree that strawberry picking is the worst—it's one of those stereotypical jobs that 'Americans simply won't do'.

Migrants from rural Mexico, Guatemala and points even farther south will do it, however, and throughout the fields of broccoli, the groves of avocado, the strawberry patches and the grape vines, you can often hear indigenous dialects— *P'urhépecha, Alagüilac, Chibchan*—lilting languages that pre-date Columbus.

To Emiliano, the grape harvest will be an easy couple of months—he'll put in fifty hours, ten per day, and earn five hundred dollars, the bulk of which he will send home to his wife. "I take a lot of pride in what I do," he assured me in a Guadalajaran dialect that resembles Castilian Spanish. "I wouldn't do anything else. I'm outdoors, we are all friends and rarely is there any problems with the vineyard owners. They seem to understand that the work we do is tough."
He compared agricultural work to the other options available to him—for instance, piece work in one of the brutal border-

town *maquiladoras* paying around 40 pesos a day along with a weekly bonus of food coupons worth 55 pesos. In the current economy, a peso is worth about eight cents. The Mexican unions provide a yearly wage increase, but local shops know it and raise prices accordingly; water is almost beyond what people can afford, meat is essentially non-existent on the dinner table, and milk is a luxury purchased only if there are children.

"Legal rights?" he scoffed. "So much ink on paper."

That's why back-breaking , subsistence-wage-paying, nomadic migrant work is preferable to living in poverty beneath a Mexican factory, which may or may not close next year because of competition from the even more brutal Chinese.

Me, I last but a single day in the vineyard. Okay, a morning. Well, part of a morning, anyway; a few rows. After that, I pull journalistic rank and skedaddled with a beefed-up Tundra, bed loaded with grapes to the crusher as if I 'needed' to write that story, which I didn't.

Not that anyone gives a shit anyway — once the novelty of making fun of my Spanish and asking me, "*Listo para el contrato* — Ready for the contract?" wears off, it is obvious how far behind the others my pickage skills are lagging.

I am, in fact, the Weakest Link. *Goodbye.*

THE JAMES GANG :
JESSE, DEAN & TOBIN

For some reason, I have had an aberrant fascination with Jesse James since I was a kid. I have visited all the landmarks of his life story, I fictionalized him in my first, sad little Western (written when I was a teenager and which I think sold about a dozen copies, mostly to people who share my DNA) and I named my first-born son, Jesse Martin, after him.

So, my serendipitous delight can only be imagined when I learned that Paso Robles was founded by Jesse James' uncle, and that Jesse and his wiser brother Frank spent time here.

And not only that, but were well-thought of when they did, displaying the mien of polite and hardworking gentlemen, not the psychopathy of the wanted desperadoes that they had, by that time, become.

Mike Harris, a seventh generation Roblan who volunteers at the quaint, comfortable Paso Robles Historical Society on 12th Street, walks me through the story of Drury Woodson James and his initial reluctance to welcome his reprobate nephews into his hard-won, fully legitimate California existence.

In 1857, when the brothers Blackburn (James and Daniel) purchased twenty-five thousand acres of northern San Luis Obispo county from a Mexican soldier called Penilo Ríos, it was the domain of Salinian Indians, kit foxes and whatever thermophile found the hundred degree water of the local hot springs habitable. They divvied up the plot, with Daniel keeping the portion of land upon which the city of Paso Robles now stands.

In 1868, Drury W. James purchased a half-interest in Daniel's holding.

James had followed the money to California during the Gold Rush nearly twenty years before and had found a far more lucrative calling: Beef. The gold was elusive to all but the luckiest miner, but successful or not, they were always hungry and with little access to fresh meat, they were willing to pay top dollar for it—and in a literal sense: Beef sold for upwards of a buck a pound; not a bad return-on-investment for Mr. James considering that cattle could be had for twenty dollars a head.

So, instead of panning, Drury James started ranching.

In 1860, having soothed his weary drover bones in the Paso Robles hot spring, he bought a nearby ten thousand acre ranch called La Panza and decided to stay. His business grew, and by the time he picked up the property from Blackburn (including the hot springs), he was a very wealthy, very canny businessman; La Panza Ranch had its own post office, tavern and restaurant.

And about that time, his infamous nephews decided to drop in. At the time, Jesse was suffering the lingering effects of a gunshot wound, although accounts differ as to whether he received it while trying to surrender to Union cavalry near Lexington, Missouri or during the robbery of the Russellville, Kentucky bank.

Whatever the cause, the healing mineral waters of Paso Robles beckoned for several reasons, not the least of which is they were many, many miles from the posses that would soon come sniffing around for them.

Drury James was not delighted at the prospect of a visit; he was aware, of course, that his nephews were wanted men, and he was from a different generation; he'd fought proudly under Zachary Taylor in Mexico and was now perhaps the wealthiest man in Central California. He was a dandified country squire, and his brothers (including Jesse's father Robert) were Baptist ministers.

History does not record what caused him his change of heart, but a good guess might include the strong 'blood is blood' loyalty among Southern families that later saw Frank James acquitted of murder in Independence, Missouri with a jury made up of relatives and friends. The foreman is said to have announced the verdict without deliberation: "We find the defendant Alexander Franklin James guilty. *Of nothing.*"

And yet, throughout their time in Paso Robles, the James brothers behaved as quiet and respectful guests at La Panza ranch. Local lore insists that they hid out for a while in a nearby cave, but offers no reason why they were compelled to do so. More interesting is the fact that the cave was used for the same purpose by another desperado, a horse thief named 'Peachy' — later hanged in Paso Robles — after whom the many of the area's 'Peachy' references, including Peachy Canyon Winery, are named. Peaches, as it happen, do not grow here.

While in Paso, Frank and James lent their shoulders to a number of local building projects, including the home of the town's co-founder, Daniel Blackburn. Their stay predates Uncle Drury's biggest accomplishment, the Paso Robles Hotel, which he built for $160,000. It was by far the most magnificent hotel between Los and Angeles and San Francisco, and rooms could go for more than two hundred dollars per night. It burned to the ground in 1940 and in the pre-War, post-Depression economy, it was not rebuilt: Reconstruction estimates were in the range of $31 million.

Neither Frank nor Jesse James returned to California; Jesse

was murdered in 1882 by a fortune-hungry gang member in a double-cross that has been written about extensively in Americana literature.

What is perhaps less well known is that after his brother's death and his stroke of fortune in Independence, Frank James saw the light; the Tacoma Times reported in July, 1914, a year before he died, that he was working as a simple, honest farm hand, never having had another brush with the law.

***

Within the annals of the eerie, two almost inconceivably bizarre images come to mind:

First, the photograph of John Lennon signing Mark David Chapman's copy of *Double Fantasy* hours before Chapman shot him to death.

The second is the brief black-and-white reel of James Dean's public service announcement made at the end of an episode of *Warner Bros. Presents* meant to plug the release of Dean's upcoming film *Giant*. Responding to host Gig Young's questions about his sudden obsession with car racing, Dean ad-libbed the following advice to young people:

"Take it easy driving; the life you save may be mine."

Thirteen days later, on September 30, 1955, at the intersection of Route 466 (now CA 46) and Route 41, Dean was killed in a head-on car crash that was, by all accounts, the fault of the other guy—a Cal Poly student with the unlikely name of

Turnupseed.

At the time of his death, Dean was a popular star, but hardly a cultural icon. In fact, two of his legacy films (and there are only three), *Giant* and the persona-defining *Rebel Without A Cause*, were released after he died, and he remains the only Hollywood legend to have received more posthumous acting award nominations than pre-humous ones.

Dying, as the wags like to quip, was a good career move. He was twenty-four years old.

On that fateful night, James Dean and his German mechanic Rolf Wütherich were traveling on then-Route 466, heading west toward Paso Robles, where they were slated to have dinner with a couple of Dean's racing buddies. All were ultimately aimed toward Salinas, intending to compete in a road race that weekend.

Dean was driving the now infamous *'Little Bastard'*, a tiny, aluminum-bodied 1955 Porsche 550 Spyder he had bought a week before with his proceeds from his *East of Eden*, and at $7000, the purchase likely took the entire kit and kaboodle.

In another macabre premonition, upon viewing the car, British actor Alec Guinness shook his head and told him: "If you get in that car, you will be found dead in it by this time next week."

And exactly seven days later, he was. Wrong place, wrong time, wrong everything.

Twenty miles from Paso Robles, at around six in the evening, the Porche passed the Y-shaped junction at Cholame and was struck nearly head-on by Turnupseed's lumbering Tudor coupe; the student was making a left turn and failed to see the low-profile sports car in the failing light. Dean himself took the brunt of the crash and died of a broken neck on the way to the Paso Robles War Memorial Hospital; Turnupseed was only slightly injured, but Wütherich, who was ejected from the car, considerably more so.

For perspective, Wütherich survived the crash but not its psychological endowment: He soon fell into a pattern of heavy drinking and was unable to hold a steady job and himself died in a drunken auto accident a few years later.

Not so Turnupseed, who went on to turn the family electrical business into a multimillion-dollar empire—he died of cancer in 1995, but his odd Burpee-esque moniker can be seen on re-wound motors to this day.

That almost unfathomably unlucky instant, which amplified the 'Live Fast, Die young and Leave a Good-Looking Corpse' rallying cry that empowered generations of rebels—with or without causes, and who James Dean, in retrospect, probably would have rejected—remains preserved in cultural amber.

The interchange has been re-routed a few hundred yards northwest, the nitrate on East of Eden has begun to deteriorate and to upwardly mobile millennials, the name 'Jimmy Dean' may connote more sizzling sausage than smoldering sexuality. But to those of us from another era, that horrific scream of metal impacting metal, the smell of blood on dirt, the useless tug of speculation remains as keen and relevant as any tragedy before or since.

Also suspended in prehistoric animation is Cholame's Jack's Ranch Café, a quarter mile from the crash site. It was certainly open when the shit came down at the nearby junction because it lays claim to having 'the oldest drive-thru window' in Central California, dating from the turn of the twentieth century.

The music loop playing when I stopped in could have been playing the day that Dean died — moldering country tunes with twangy lyrics, where, in *'I'm-a jest a rollin' stone, and I keep on traveling on…'*, the word 'stone' rhymes with the word 'on'. The sign above the cash register reads *'Today's menu; take it or leave it'* and even the plastic sunflowers in the vase look dead.

But Dean could have known none of this — he died a thousand yards before he would have passed Jack's Ranch Café.

Nonetheless, the place is decked out in James Dean paraphernalia; *'Boulevard of Broken Dreams'* posters, coffee mugs emblazoned with James Dean's mug, *'4-Ever Cool'* license plate holders, a rack with ten different types of post cards but all of James Dean.

The staff speaks so affectionately of him that he might have been born in a manger out back and I'm half-tempted to ask the oldsters if they can share any Dean stories — and equally, expect them to say, 'Yeah, ol' Jimmy, that little whippersnapper — he'd go and break his damn fool neck *ever' time he passed this way…'*

The landscape through which James Dean sped, this very time of year, is proudly desiccated and savagely beautiful; as stark and subtle as Cal Trask. From a distance, the buttes and pastures look barren, but become wildly fertile when nurtured from stream water or the many artesian aquifers with which the county is blessed.

As it is somewhat cursed with hot springs. Cursed because — commercial *ka-chinging* and made-up health benefits aside — geothermal groundwater is volcanic in nature, and here you are standing on ground zero of the most famous transform fault on earth, the San Andreas.

Carrying much of the California coast and all of Baja along with it, the Pacific plate is pile-driving northward at a rate that might have had James Dean pulling out his hair — but keeping him alive to do it — two inches per year, and every once in a while decides to have a grand mal seizure like the one it did in 1906, causing the greatest loss of life from a natural disaster in California's history.

But that *is* history. Throughout fifteen thousand years of pre-history, the T'epoy'aha'l tribe, who used the Dean death route as a hunting corridor, must have experienced many earthquakes; seismologists claim that megathrust quakes above 8 in magnitude — where one of the earth's tectonic plates is thrust under another — happen every few hundred years.

Without buildings to collapse, earthquake damage done to 'The People of the Oak' was likely minimal and probably resulted in nothing more substantial than fable fodder to be passed through the generations via the songs of elders.

Geophysicists predict that the fault is overdue for another massive temper tantrum, but whether it will most devastate Los Angeles or San Francisco is a prediction that no one is willing make. One thing is certain, though: Regardless of this quake's epicenter, many more will follow as the Pacific Plate continues its inexorable ride northward and the neighboring North American Plate, bearing the rest of the United States on its back, slides south.

In fifteen million years or so, Los Angeles will be closer to San Francisco than is Oakland — a scenario that should piss off residents of both cities more than the temporary trembles.

This steady grinding of mantle rock against mantle rock, like the grinding of Turnupseed's Ford and Dean's Porche, is essential time perspective. Because, however much it seems so, nothing is really preserved in amber, and any other overview of our lives, James Dean's life, the Jack Creek Café smorgasbord of the macabre, is pure illusion.

***

Prior to my visit, when more than a couple people warned me to watch out for Tobin James because 'he's a real *cowboy*', I sort of braced myself. Because in my grasp of 2013 parlance, a 'real cowboy' means that breed of overstuffed stud who seems obligated to squeeze every drop of testosterone from his endocrine system and smear it all over his ego.

I've met a few and I trust that you have too.

Instead, I encounter a *real* cowboy; the luck-wishers had simply placed the emphasis on the wrong word.

Or at least, Tobin James turns out to be a character I believe to be in lock-step with the real character of real cowboys from real days of real yore: Individualists who were not particularly comfortable in the spotlight, who, being somewhat off-key, self-effacing and pragmatic, did not blow their own horns easily.

Of course, with the mule kick of a few shots of rye under their belt buckles, the tall tales might fly; the volume of the conversation might rise, personalities might inflate and the horsepucky might begin to hit the overhead fan — and in this, Tobin James is also right on cue.

Neither intimidating, overbearing nor pompous, Tobin

James — to nail it all to the wall in a single word — is likeable. It's high noon: The sprawling tasting room along Highway 46, about eight miles east of Paso, is crowded and I ask Tobin James if it's normally this busy so early in the day.

"Busy?" he answers, genuinely puzzled. "This is sort of slow."

He points to the 1860s Brunswick mahogany bar: "Come back in a couple hours — you'll barely find a spot."

I do and I didn't, but James prefers to talk on the porch anyway, away from the madcap crowd. I don't object — the tasting room is too raucous for repartee.

Decked out like a cornball hodgepodge Dodge City saloon, the sheer exuberance of the tasting room patrons saves it from being totally obnoxious — that and the fact that it is built on the site of a genuine nineteenth century stagecoach stop. Plus, it serves as a kitschy counterweight to the austere formality of a few nearby wineries I could name, and a lot of people come for the fun, if not the education.

"We couldn't figure out how to do snobby," James points out. "So we did 'friendly' instead."

Tobin James has a wine pedigree — he was raised up to his paisley cowpoke bandanna in it, albeit in a place you probably wouldn't free-associate with wine: Indiana, where the cool, wet climate is the antithesis of Central California Mediterranean near-desert conditions.

But he had a brother who owned a vineyard and another brother who owned a wine store, and when, as a young man, he opted to heed Horace Greeley's advice and go west, he had winemaking on his mind. He started off as an unpaid cellar rat, willing to do anything to learn the craft, and when his ship came in, it had four wheels on the bottom and a flatbed on top loaded with grapes — and a future father-in-law at the helm.

And the grapes were free. Apparently, a local fruit monger called Laz Morones had a customer who reneged on a deal to buy six tons of zinfandel grapes and was looking to unload them quickly and painlessly since, as he put it, 'I can't put 'em back on the vine.'

At the time, James was working for our old pal Gary Eberle, and back then, Gary was not interested in making zin and passed on the opportunity. Somewhat gingerly, Tobin asked Eberle if he could take the harvest himself and use the winery's equipment to make his own batch of wine, his first.

And in a show of Paterno paternalism such as had jump-started his own self-confidence, Eberle agreed.

One could use the hackneyed catchphrase 'the rest is history', but as it happens, that batch itself made history. It won two double gold medals, and two years later, in 1989, Tobin James launched his own enterprise, Peachy Canyon Winery.

In 1992, eight years after he'd entered the fray, Tobin James wore a pretty proud crown: Peachy Canyon 'Westside' Zinfandel 1990 ended up as number 69 on Wine Spectator's Top 100 Wines of the World.

In the world of intangibles, wine people use (and just as often, misuse) the term *terroir* as a consummation devoutly to be wished. This 'essence of place', all-important in tight little French wine communities — as it is by default in tight little French-wannabe wine communities — is bounced around elsewhere in this book. For now, I am considering a similar wine phenomenon, this one made of DNA instead of dirt and involving more psychology than geology, more sociology than topography. That is, how a winemaker's personality is reflected in the personality of the wine he produces.

Characterroir, if you will.

In other words, we know that a clone from Château de Pommard makes a different wine in Oregon, but we also know that the same clone made a different wine in 1943 Burgundy than it does in 2013 Burgundy. Same basic climate, same grape, same pedigreed estate. Different *vigneron.*

Tobin James still speaks with syrupy nostalgia about his first, prizewinning zinfandel; he chases that raspberry-and-chocolate-flavored dragon to this day.

And I get it: It doesn't matter how many doctorates your kid earns, you'll still look wistfully at your photo of their first day of kindergarten, won't you?

And it is that first, wonderful kindergarten wine — done *sua sponte* as the lawyers say — that Tobin seeks to recreate in every vintage. And succeeds more often than he may realize. Tobin James not only splashes his name across the label, it seems to hold some of his private essence inside — and not in a banal way, like perfume manufacturers do with celebrity fragrances. For example, when they released Paris Hilton's 'Siren', Parlux said, *'It's all about being playful in a sexy way!'* and when Gigantic created 'Purr' for Katy Perry, reviews said *'Opens with pretty notes and ends with a relatively generic bottom'.*

Katy herself gushed nonsensically and somewhat genie-ishly, *'It's basically* me *inside a bottle.'*

Frankly, I can live without a noseful of Katy Perry, but I find Tobin James' redolent reds to be frontier-styled and larger-than-life; explosive with weight and saturated with in-your-face assertiveness.

But, like Tobin — and his fellow Jameses, Jesse and Dean — there is a lot of cool stuff going on within the subterranean fathoms: A startling delicacy and a sense not only of place but of resolve. The fundamental fruit in a classic Tobin James vintage like 2007 is never stewed or jammy; it tastes bright and freshly picked. The cascade of liquid cocoa is hedonism certainly, but the exuberance is reined by a moody hint of earth and leather. There are scents of raspberry, but also a myriad of subtle spices braiding through. The top-heavy tone is tempered by a touch of tenuto, the concupiscence calmed by contemplation.

Like Tobin James.

There was something abut him that struck me then, and something that moves me to this day: Several times in our conversation, James brought up the word 'estrella' — Spanish for 'star', the name of the first winery at which he apprenticed as well as his vineyards' watershed, the Estrella River. And every time he said it, he pronounced it correctly, like the Mexicans do, softening the double 'l' into a single 'y'. And afterward, he re-pronounced it the way his Anglo neighbors do, like I do — which is to say, wrong.

To me, somebody who is willing to risk bogging down the chit-chat to make an accommodating cultural point displays a lot of inborn respect for his surroundings, his milieu, his terroir.

It's part of Tobin James' *characterroir*, and it's a small thing to be sure. But small things are what rumble the foundation of charisma; they are what I sniff for in a glass of zinfandel, a ramekin of olive oil, a tulip of craft-made gin and, yeah, in the character of a winemaking cowboy with his shit-kickers propped up on a hitching post in Wild, Wild Paso Robles.

ALEXIS' ATTITUDE & ZIN ZEN

Describing Stillman's outfit one evening, Alexis — Stillman's long-time live-in squeeze — speaks with easy, pointed grace. Fashion sense is one of her congenital endowments:

"Today, Mr. Brown is coutured in a brocade, champagne-colored tuxedo trimmed in black velveteen over an embroidered paisley print shirt in ecru and aubergine. His Pendleton trousers are green and blue tartan, patterned after kilts from the Clan Gordon; his shoes, which he insists on calling 'clown shoes' to go with his pompadour, are in fact caramel-colored slip-on loafers. His ensemble is color-complimented by the glass of syrah he is holding and by his platinum ice hair."

Now, I may not be José Ibar, but if I believe that platinum ice hair complements ecru and plaid, I may as well be José Feliciano.

In any event, the flesh fails the foppery. Fifty-six years and a lifetime of California sun and living like a rock star on a Poli Sci major's budget has tinted him bronze and left him slightly corrugated. One of this sons recently told him that he looks like a wallet, and he repeated this story to me several times, more amused at the kid's acuity than insulted by it. He has the temperament of political pundit, questionable (at best) business sense, the sort of grim saltiness of a middle-aged metal and punk-lovin' beach bum and possesses the uncanny ability to discern infinitesimal changes in a fermenting vat of grape juice — unusual, because he smokes like a tire fire; cigars, menthol cigarettes (mostly borrowed) and that squirrely stuff for which you need a prescription — both are habits that usually require you to cash in your taste buds. Stillman Brown may wear look-at-me suits, talk about his dick a lot and come across in a social setting somewhat less polished than his toenails, but this should not dissuade you understanding that he is very, very bright. Brighter than me, anyway. As a kid he could name every senator in Congress and probably can today; he blew through Berkeley, wowing professors who figured that his career path was either academia or spook work in Washington D.C.

"I didn't have the language skills to work for the CIA," he declares. "And I didn't have the discipline to be a scholar. All I wanted was the carefree life of a drug dealer, and you see, now I have it."

Beside the Elvis books, his coffee table is loaded with boring smart-people periodicals like *The Economist* and *The Wall Street Journal* that he reads cover-to-cover as soon as each issue arrives.

At Stillman's birthday bash, I briefly meet a man who claims to have raised him — his step-father — a long-haired, nearly wheelchair-bound old fellow named Dan who mentions Stillman in passing, then goes on at length about Janis Joplin and what has become of other members of Big Brother And The Holding Company — a subject which holds my interest about as long as *The Economist.*

For some reason, like Stillman, Dan has a habit of switching locomotives mid-track, and in the middle of the Joplin story, he begins to recount, in excruciating detail, some funny cartoon he'd seen in *Playboy* many, many, many years ago.

Which, by a million to one chance, I'd seen too and remember clearly, but I hold my tongue when he screws up the punch line, opting to take further notes on the Swilly story not from Dan, but from the sputum spouter himself.

Stillman Brown was conceived on New Year's Eve in Fresno, or so he postulates. His parents were students at California State University, his mother finishing up a biology degree and his father, having left a government gig in Greenland, had just enrolled there; he'd met the future Mrs. Brown somewhere on campus, did the ol' blanket drill after a night of doing whatever folks did in the fifties on New Year's Eve before they had sex.

Dad went on to be a corporate financial whiz at PepsiCo and his mother a schoolteacher.

Or something like that. With Stillman, you have to hear several versions of any story before you can even dream of throwing a dart at the elusive target of truth. Over the course of our month together, he tells me at various times that his father was a reclusive billionaire with really long fingernails, a fireman who saved a bunch of lives on 9/11, a black Delta blues singer from Vicksburg and the son of Jesse Garon Presley, who, it develops, did not die at childbirth after all.

One thing is certain: Dan did not raise him, but emerged as his mother's husband and his erstwhile business partner ("We fiddle-fucked around for a decade until it became clear that Dan couldn't sell armor-piercing ammo to a street gang") when Stillman was in his twenties. Somehow, even so, Stillman has managed to inherit Dan's sense of the phantasmagorical.

As you may have guessed, the Elvis idolization and attendant psychosis is strict dramaturgical shtick, neither indigestible nor ungovernable, and Stillman, by his own admission, doesn't even like Elvis that much. But getting him to say that in polite society is the hard sell—it's like trying to get Kiss to appear without make-up back in the day or finding out some meditation maven's secret mantra.

In fact, all he's willing to give up is, "You know how to most Elvis impersonators, it's 80% tongue-in-cheek? To me, it's 102% tongue-in-cheek, but it helps me proselytize about what kinds of drugs to avoid and which to embrace. Elvis never was a wine drinker, you know."

Intense and nicotine-stained with Sartre's pragmatic nihilism, the one subject about which Stillman does not often stray into the realm of the surreal is winemaking, where the devil, along with the deity, is in the details. He obsesses over them in the middle of the night, chain-smokes when he can't work out a technical issue, and retains a thread of mental distance at all times during a conversation, like a junkie or an autistic kid, trying to hold up his end of the exchange when his head is really inside the zinfandel vat, nose to the bunghole, trying to figure out why — many, many hours after stirring in the Fermaid K — the intransigent must hovers at 6% alcohol. Tasting it, this is one of those times when the phrase, 'This is fucking *sweet!*' is a pejorative.

Back inside the land of the giants — 15,000-gallon steel-jacked fermentation tanks — his handful of barrels may be dwarfed by volume, but not by purpose. Each cask slumbers in various stages of restless ontogeny; simmering, stewing, murmuring, purring, gently modifying its behavior because of human nudgings, because of the machinery of nature, because of countless tiny contrivances on which we really do not have a grasp or else building a syrah would be like building a Subaru.

Our vermentino (I use a proprietary 'our' now because my palm oil was crushed along with the berries) sits in a Transtore storage tank, twenty-four hours into morphogenesis; it looks like a foamy sea of butterscotch soda.

A gigantic, skull-filling whiff at the tank top reveals evolution just as an erudite sniff of a wine glass of final product will, but here, instead vermentino's characteristic peppery lime and green apple nose, the baby batch smells of sulphur, acid and various sharp volatiles that are in process of fermenting out.

Nonetheless, there is nothing off in the odor, nothing to suggest that all those fine-spun flavors will not emerge on schedule, and Stillman pronounces it 'adorable'.

It takes an experienced palate and an active imagination to taste this raw juice and predict a future. A novice like me can't do it — any more than I can look at a tube of paint and envision the Sistine Chapel.

Today, the focus is again on the pinot noir. Two tons of it are sitting in T-Bins, ready to be pressed.

At this time of year, Paso Robles Wine Services is up to its neck in gators (mostly instigators, promulgators and mitigators) and equipment is what it is, but the pressing appointment is pressing; it has to be carefully planned to coincide with the precise coming-of-age cotillion ball that strange, sensuous pinot noir demands.

Time it wrong, she throws a hissy fit.

Pinot noir, of course, is the baroness of Burgundy; the wine world's equivalent to a rock star whose contract rider refuses brown M&Ms in the dressing room. I've seen the varietal described as 'fickle' a thousand times, but fickleness implies caprice — that is, a sort of callous disregard for those mooning saps who want to possess her. I don't see pinot noir that way. Stately and stubborn, the grape may be high-maintenance and tough to tame, but given precise conditions — some ordained, others modified — it produces wine that is as loyal to her infatuates as they are to her. She's not off to Monaco to marry a Prince and abandon her calling; she remains upon the silver screen, beautiful in balance, filled with gutsy gossamer, equal parts coyness, courtliness and carnality.

A two-story tall Diemme AR-80 MSC press looms in the PRWS side lot, a bit larger than the operation requires, but it's all that's available.

The grapes have now fermented dry and are holding a relative acidity pH of 3.6; tannins are supple, soft and sensuous (clone 777 may occasionally produce clumsy tannins, but not here), the fruit explosive and the alcohol-by-volume—even humbled by Jesus Juice—remains high, but not stupidly so for Paso pinot: Slightly below 16%.

And that *is* Paso pinot, baby: Big stuff.

Into the axial feeder it goes, bins lifted by a hi-lo and shoveled into the maw by minimum-wage grunts.

That's cool: Like watching artisan manchego coagulating with juice from sheep stomachs or *foie gras* geese being force-fed corn mush, when you stand on the ground floor of wine wizardry, witnessing the man behind the curtain sometimes reveals zits and pustule-guts, and if you don't want to see them, keep a tight hold on Toto.

Some things should not be seen, but they should still be tasted. And immediately, too. Internally, the Diemme pneumatic press has a rubber membrane programmed to run through cycles of inflation; every time it does, free run, pomegranate-colored juice pours from the beast's underbelly and into a steel basin. From there it is pumped into a portable tank, but first—after each of the eight cycles—the wine is given (by Stillman and anyone else who happens to be hanging around) an organoleptic, objective analysis. A taste test, in other words. And with each pressing, the quality of the flavor morphs, becoming less brittle, less fierce, less imbued with strange, evanescent seed phenolics, richer and more elegant in depth. Already present, if still nubile and lurking behind unlovely words like *catechin* and *epicatechin*, *monomeric anthocyanin* and *diethyl disulphide* (all will quickly fade) are the culinary descriptors we are fond of using with fine pinot noir: Ripe tomato, mushroom, cinnamon, black cherry.

It's a far cry from what a year in barrels will do to it, of course. And the final stage of the day's work, presumably the last one prior to bottling, is transferring the wine from the steel tanks into *limousin* casks procured from fellow winemaker Dan Tudor.

These barrels were prepped in advance — staves tightened, body filled with water and allowed to stew for a spell to prevent too much wine from being sucked up into the wood. Within this cocoon of oak, as in a time capsule, it will excogitate, grow, 'find itself' for a year or so.

Like any beauty with a soul, pinot noir needs some breathing space.

Stillman treats his wine like progeny, not a lover: "As long as the chemistry stays within a certain stable parameter *[as long as the kid stays out of jail]* I'm not out to create the tastiest *[smartest]*, most awarded *[Pulitzer Peace Prize followed by canonization]* pinot noir the world has ever known. I'm after not after an ideal *[the Christ child]*, I'm after a wine with personality *[a kid you like to hang around with]*.

Stillman has three adult sons — Luke, Jake and John (Biblical names all) — and they are awfully fun to hang around with. They are each as smart and cynical as their old man, and they see right through my personal, scattershot method of trying to leave an impression on people, which includes using big words and lousy improv jokes. Like Stillman, they don't suffer posers gladly, but recognize sincerity, even couched in the applesauce of pretention, and that's why they roll their eyes at the pink, the velvet, the Elvis and love the old dude to the ends of the earth.

Alexis, too. She met him in the early nineties when she as still married to her second husband; they bonded over a strange gang of wine-loving outdoors-types called The Southwest Adventurers and Gourmet Society who referred to themselves as 'Swaggarts' in homage to the hooker-hoppin' television evangelist of the era. They used to hang out in gorgeous places like Aspen and the north rim of the Grand Canyon, hiking, camping, drinking great wine and cooking great food over wood fires.

According to Alexis, the Graceland craze began around this time, spearheaded by a guy who takes it even further than Stillman: He's wholesale wine merchant from Sedona currently D.B.A his *nom de spume* Elvis Kokopelli, although he has so many aliases that I wouldn't dream of trying to list them all. Leave it at *'Chief of the Dream Police of the Medicine Wheel of Fortune; the Roustabout Reincarnation of King Elvis Everywhere.'*

As for Alexis Louise, for all her lithe charm, vogue chutzpah and blame-avoidance for the Memphis-Meltdown motif (she seems to actually dig Elvis music), she must nonetheless accept responsibility for the rococo cuckoo Stillman Style, which (as a proud Midwestern schlub) I submit as being Pre-Bill Belew Southern Christian Boy Rock 'n' Roll Rebel fused with Vintage Slacker Skatepop Tremolo-Picking Surf Vortex SoCal Punk.

If I have missed the point, it may be because missing the point *is* the point.

Through her trenchant eye, however, Stillman has proven

once again—as did the pomaded Kaiser of Kitsch in 1956—that although pink and black don't mix, don't blend and don't coalesce, they work.

"Yes," she *mea culpas,* her pretty face behind the confessional screen turning what L'Oréal calls Fandango Crimson:

"I am indeed his wardrobe mistress. He allows me to dress him. He's good natured that way."

You are absolved of this, Alexis: *Et ego te absolvo a peccatis tuis in nomine Patris, et Fili, et Spiritus Sancti.* Go and sin no more.

So, Alexis' penance is to say no Hail Marys, no Our Fathers, no Acts of Contrition, but to describe (in forty words or less) the fashion fusion that best reflect her own edgy essence:

"This evening, I am wearing a 1960's cranberry red silk evening gown with jet beads layered over a monkey tee and accessorized with motorcycle boots. What takes this ensemble from grocery store work to the Old Cayucos Tavern? Attitude."

Cuckoo Castles: Hearst & Eagle

Listen my children and you shall hear,
Of erstwhile egos exploded here,
On 46 West and then again
Above the park, San Simeon.
For Hearst and Stemper, shed no tear.

There are a few things money can't buy you, my children. Among them are love, loyalty, luck and aesthetic responsibility.

Far be it from me to second guess somebody with millions of dollars in disposable income, but San Luis Obispo County's two most prominent eyesores may as well have been designed by Albert Speer with a nasty hangover. Like the megalomaniacal, would-be Eighth Wonder of the World *Große Halle* Speer designed for Germania — Hitler's plan for Europe — the two local hilltop edifices Eagle Castle and Hearst's Castle have everything a homeowner could want...

Except a sense of scale.

In 1919, having built the lowly, failing *San Francisco Examiner* into the nation's largest newspaper chain, having invented yellow journalism while serving two terms in the House of Representatives, William Randolph Hearst surveyed his wild, beautiful, undeveloped Rancho Piedra Blanca above the blue Pacific and said (or something similar): "Wouldn't a fifty-six bedroom, sixty-one bath mansion with a movie theater, an airfield and the world's largest private zoo simply *make* the place?"

Designed by Julia Morgan, Hearst Castle—formally named '*La Cuesta Encantada*'—sits, in all its surreal grandeur, on a quarter million acres of cattle country about forty miles west of Paso Robles. It has to be seen to be disbelieved. Pieced together from bits of European architecture, including ceilings from churches and monasteries and an ancient Roman temple front, transported wholesale from Italy and reconstructed at the site, an architect might keep a straight face in referring to this overdone Baroque behemoth as 'eclectic'. Over 90,000 square foot of building space, a private power plant, 127 acres of gardens, nineteen drawing rooms and a swimming pool holding 345,000 gallons of water fed by spring water piped in from the Santa Lucia Mountains.

Hearst frequently stopped in the nearby town of Harmony for buttermilk on his way to the castle, where he must have caused quite a stir; in 1920, Harmony had a population of 10. Today, that number has swelled to 18.

A sense of scale is one thing, but what about a sense of humor?

I opt out of taking a tour of Hearst Castle, as tempting as it is to spend $25 worth of hard-earned cash to gawk at someone else's hard-earned cash. I choose instead to wander around the souvenir room and take photographs of the photographs of the 16th century tapestries, the Doge's suite, the colonnades and Cassou statues and Roman baths.

I do not, it may be noted, purchase anything. Not the Hearst Castle logo key chains, two for $6; not the Hearst Castle logo pennies—$1.01 each; not the Hearst Castle logo Christmas tree ornaments, t-shirts, hoodies, visors, cloches or the inexplicable Hearst Castle logo *Indiana Jones* hats.

As for Hearst's sense of humor — and lack thereof — since everybody knows that Xanandu in *Citizen Kane* was patterned after Hearst Castle — just as Kane was the embodiment of Hearst the man — and since the entire rationale for this cheesy operation is to fleece nickels and dimes from tourists, why are no gee-gaws with a nod to Orson Welles?

Not even in hawking Hearst Ranch Wine, the estate's pet project, do the Hearst heirs opt for a cute tagline like, *'We Will Sell No Wine Before Its Time'*.

Perhaps because to them, it is no laughing matter: William Random Hearst detested the *film à clef* so much that he forbade his publications from mentioning it, which is one of the reasons why *Citizen Kane* failed to recoup its costs at the box office at the time of its release. Hearst went so far as to contact Hollywood executives like Louis B. Mayer to try and purchase the film's negatives in order to burn them.

Close, but no cigar — although it would be nearly a quarter-century before Welles was given due credit for having made what is arguably the most iconic film of all time.

So, come on, State of California, who has owned the property since 1957, forgive and forget and flip a buck: A little red pinewood sled with the Hearst Castle logo stamped about 'Rosebud'?

That I'd pay twenty-five dollars for.

No tours at any price can be had at Eagle Castle, even though the sign out front says that the tasting room is 'open daily' and the massive limestone fortress is available for weddings. I'm turned away by a sentry at the gate once it becomes clear that my name does not appear on the registry for that day's round of 'meetings'.

More mystery surrounds this crenellated chimera (which actually makes Hearst Castle look like a pastiche of sensitive landscaping) than Area 51, and locals close ranks and exchange glances when you ask about it; I feel like Jonathan Harker asking Transylvanian villagers for directions to Count Dracula's crumbling manor. Roblan rustics do everything but cross themselves as they dodge my inquiries.

I have no doubt that legal wrangles lie at the parochial core of the provincial code of small-town secrecy, most of which will likely be wrangled out before these words see ink. But in the meantime, the lore is legion. Some folks claim the citadel is in escrow, others claim it's for sale, still others claim it's already been sold, and they know who to, but refuse to name names.

For now, as far , as I can tell, the blinding-white castle on a hilltop overlooking Highway 46 stands stark, stupendous and sterile, built of tacky ticky-tacky and more taste-free than Gallo Chenin Blanc. Its kitsch raised to the power of three.

And consider that said description is kinder than most. For posterity—and for posterity alone—I record several conversations among Roblans who were more a trifle more callous in their portrayal of Eagle Castle:

"A terrible idea executed terribly. For half the cash they could have built a stunning Spanish hacienda; instead, they wound up this cluster-fuck. If your sole goal for a winery was to fail unconditionally, you'd wind up with Eagle Castle."

And: *"Americans may be dumb sometimes and prone to doing dumb stuff, but everyone recognizes a miniature golf course when they see one. These guys apparently did not."*

And: *"The only conceivable way this place will ever turn a profit is if it sells to Hollywood who will blow it up at the end of some low-*

budget vampire flick."

And perhaps most cruel of all was the irate Yelper who described it as: *"Disney on acid; the sort of place that attracts Winnebagos filled with fat people with fat children."*

What little I can learn, I crib together from whispered sources who decline to be named, but who have actually been inside.

'Mark', for example, received a sought-after invitation to the Eagle Castle grand opening and, having watched the raising of the concrete castle walls block by block, attended the reception with some trepidation. "When too much money meets wine," he believes, "the results are often in the realm of a disaster flick."

Crash and burn, in other words. And Mark was a fan to begin with. He recalls when Eagle Castle first started selling wine in a strip mall tasting room on East 46, the wines were spectacular.

This sort of sincere, if plebian setting seemed sufficient to showcase the wares—a fruit-fueled and approachable style without searing acidity or puckery tannins, very emblematic of the user-friendly Paso path to winemaking.

There's an adage that's often quoted at the kind of weddings hosted here. It comes from 1 Corinthians 13 and runs like this:

'Love is patient, love is kind. It does not envy, it does not boast, it is not proud.'

It is a Biblical passage toward which God might have pointed Eagle Castle founder Gary Stemper when He deigned to speak to the former Paso Robles mayor and long time businessman.

At least, that's the way Mark remembers it: "During the

reception, when the giant chessboards, the suits of armor, the flying buttresses and the bagpipe player had gotten a little 'much', I stepped out to the patio and overheard Stemper telling guests that *'God instructed me to build this place'*.

If so, it was a God with somewhat limited foresight, or else Stemper took a good idea and went batshit with the envy and the pride part—the same rogue pathogen that infected William Randolph Hearst, whose original plan for his ostentatious pad was for a modest bungalow. According to a draftsman who attended the initial meeting with Julia Morgan, Hearst maintained, "I would like to build something upon the hill at San Simeon. I get tired of going up there and camping in tents; I'm getting a little too old for that. I'd like to get something that would be a little more comfortable."

In 1947, four years before he died, Hearst was evidently not yet quite comfortable enough, and work on the exhibitionistic landscape blot was still going on, twenty-eight years after it began.

To his credit, solvency lasted until the bitter end.

Not so Eagle Castle. In July, 2012, eleven years after its founding, Eagle Castle Winery LLC petitioned for Chapter 11 bankruptcy, keeping creditors at bay and creating an opportunity to restructure business affairs and assets. According to the file, those assets included — beside $375,000 in bottled wine and $132,000 in barreled wine — nearly twenty thousand dollars worth of antiques and armor.

The bulk of the cornball Camelot's $5.9 million liabilities were agribusiness loans, but the winery also owed the San Luis Obispo County tax collector about $268,000 according to a local, non-Hearstian paper, *The Tribune*.

The property was listed for sale in a trade magazine called

VineSmart for a 'reduced' price of $6.9 million, which covers the nut with a cool million to spare. The blurb calls it '*The most spectacular winery on the Central Coast*' and indicates that along with a 17,000 square foot winery and eleven acres of vines — mostly cabernet sauvignon — you'll be the proud new owner of a faux-medieval castle complete with moat and drawbridge and presumably, enough armor and recruits from local serfs to defend it.

Of course, by the time you read these words, all this sarkiness will probably be water under the above referenced drawbridge, so feel free to drop me a line and indicate how it all turned out.

If there was a liquidation sale, I would be curious if there were any little red sleds on auction.

For, borne of prodigal, profligate pelf,
Through all of our history, paeans to self
Rise only from ego, not logic or need.
The people will waken and harken the call;
The Biblical mandate, the modest man's creed:

'Pride shall goeth before the fall.'

Turning Fiji Water Into Isosceles

When Lynda and Stewart Resnick, new owners of Justin Winery, asked their on-site sommelier Jim Gerakaris for some promotional tasting notes for the next bottling of chardonnay, Jim sensed that the Beverly Hills billionaires might be ready for a learning curve: The grapes had not yet been picked.

On the other hand, when Resnick asked the estate's then winemaker and now vice president Fred Holloway what he'd do to improve product 'if he had a bottomless pocket' — which he now pretty much did — Holloway pointed out twenty acres of under-productive, poorly-spaced cabernet vines snaking up premium land on the hillside above the tasting room.

Without missing a beat he replied, "I'd rip those out and start over with a better clone, better vine spacing and new root stock."

Abracadabra: His wish wound up being the Resnicks' command.

Make no mistake, Justin Winery has always been a lovechild of cash and ego — the desire to produce wines to rival those of Bordeaux beats in the heart of every do-it-yourselfer who has ever fallen in love with one of those lyrical, lilting lovelies. But meaning well and having means to do it well is generally the road that diverges in the single wood.

Among the eight or so California wineries that changed hands in 2010, industry analysts were particularly intrigued by the sale of Justin Baldwin's 50,000 case Paso Robles property, which boasted a hotel and a restaurant along with 160 acres of vines.

Intrigued because nearly all of the other headline sales in 2010 were joints in receivership — or at least, wineries navigating stormy seas. Most of this was due to the high-tide mark reached by the sub-prime mortgage crisis — the so-called 'Great Recession' — around June of 2009.

American consumers had been steadily cutting back purchases of wines priced $30 and higher, and highly-leveraged wineries producing luxury-level wines found themselves with warehouses filled with aging, unsellable assets, and many of them could not weather the storm.

But by all accounts, Justin was doing bang-up numbers when Stewart Resnick's Roll International Corporation came sniffing around the cellar door and had, in fact, just finished up the most successful year they'd ever had. The sale was what financial linguists call 'win/win' and 'synergistic': Roll — the parent company of Fiji Water, POM Wonderful (pomegranate juice), Teleflora (flower delivery service) and Suterra, an (environmentally-friendly pesticide) — was looking to expand their large agricultural holdings into wine.

And Justin, wanting to see his thirty-year success story grow beyond what he had the dough to do alone, sold.

Interestingly, although (in his own words) Justin Baldwin was retained by the Resnicks as a sort of winery mascot — the Colonel Sanders of Justin Wines — the Justin website suggests something a bit different. Baldwin's bio is listed under 'Founder', along with a brief history of the estate he started in 1981, when Paso Robles was home to less than a dozen wineries. He'd been to France and had fallen for the supple, subtle majesty of Château Margaux and wanted to see if he could duplicate them in his own backyard. "One sip of Premier Cru and I knew I had to make my own," he says, adding, "The rewards of pioneering are greater than the risks."

As pudding proof, the bio goes on to list the jackpot glitter that has been sprinkled over the spread, including Best of Classes, Best of Regions, the Pichon Lalande trophy for 'World's Best Blended Red Wine', Wine Spectators Top 10 Wines of the World, and blah, blah, blah — Justin Baldwin himself has been one of Robert Parker Jr.'s 'Wine Heroes of the Year', a 'Star of Paso Robles', a James Beard Foundation's 'Great American Winemaker Award' and Wine Enthusiast's 'Top Cabernet and Blended Wine Producers List' for seven years running.

I did mention that Mr. Baldwin has an exuberant, extraordinary ego, right?

Now, I'd say that it is his www page, so why not? Except that it isn't. For whatever reason, the site mentions that the place is *a family owned and operated winery*, but doesn't say *whose* family, leaving the reader to assume, of course, that it is Justin Baldwin's family. Nothing whatsoever is mentioned about the change of ownership. Baldwin's deceased dogs enjoy their own page, but not the Resnicks.

And why not? I have no insider information, because my inside informer would provide none, so I can only speculate.

Could it have anything to do with the barrage of bad press that Fiji Water has battled since forming an alliance with Fiji's unelected military regime that came to power after a 2006 coup? Or the environmental impact, the plastic waste and the energy costs inherent in shipping water across thousands of miles of water so that rich Americans can avoid drinking local water? Especially since tests have shown that Fiji Water is higher in arsenic than homegrown Aquafina and Dasani — or, for that matter, Cleveland's tap water?

Or, could it relate to Fiji Water's recent threat to shut down operations in an attempt to strong-arm the government—legal or otherwise—into dropping a proposal to raise the business tax on bottled water thirty-fold?

Lest that figure seem excessive, consider that currently, Fiji Water is taxed than half a Fiji cent per liter (Fiji Water sells for about $4 per liter in California), totaling about a quarter million U.S. dollars a year. The proposed hike would generate about twenty million more in Fiji funds (about equal to their U.S. marketing budget), which is still pretty paltry when you consider that Fiji Water extracts about three million liters of public water from every month; a scenario over which the public, which is currently under martial law, has no control.

I could say that the Fiji scuttlebutt is neither here nor there, but that wouldn't be fair to Justin Winery, because the scandal is, in fact there, not here. It's there.

As it happens, the Resnicks have approached this latest venture with a lot of class and earnest money. Having grown the output (the winery now vinifies 150,000 cases annually) and gussied up the tasting room with Bauhausian brevity, Justin Winery is in the throes of such a construction boom— including a beautiful, walnut-trimmed, ceramic-tile-that-looks-like-oak floored Wine Club members-only banquet room in the barrel cellar—that tours are temporarily suspended.

Lucky for me, Jim Gerakaris offers me one anyway.

You could not find a better Justin champion than Jim; he's an elegant, deeply-knowledgeable wine and food advocate with a scholarly white goatee and a hearty belly laugh which, as in any good steward, is custom-designed for any and all off-key jokes from any and all customers.

Enough to say that none of the Fiji trash talk I just prattled on about came from his lips.

He's clearly proud of the improvements in the operation to which he's been an integral part for five years, and is fond of saying: "If you like these wines now, wait three or four vintages…"

By then, he promises, the build-outs will be completed and the newly planted vines will be coming into their own.

These vines spread splendidly across the hilly countryside at a high-end elevation of 1800 feet, part of the original 87 acres that Justin Baldwin planted in 1981.

Soils here are primarily sedimentary limestone and clay seeded with nutrients from nearby volcanic out-croppings. This was the *mise en scène* that Baldwin reckoned ideal for his Bordeaux-away-from-home scenario, up to and including Chateau Overlook that appears to have been beamed down from La Mothe de Margaux on the left bank of the Garonne. The latter site, formerly Baldwin's home, is now a wildly romantic venue for weddings.

As Gerakaris points out, these acres, though responsible for some of the highest notes in the Justin résumé, could not possibly produce sufficient crop to fill the pipeline, so very early on, Baldwin began to form partnerships with the best of Paso Robles growers. This allows a genuine cross-section of quality produce reflective of the multitude of microclimates across the appellation. Halter Ranch, for example — two miles northwest of Justin — boasts a whole new smorgasbord of soils, ayar to zaca, producing gorgeous zinfandel; Laura's Vineyard, close to Cambria, grows 20 acres of rich, expressive cabernet exclusively for Justin.

As viticulturist and vintner usually do not reside within the same *corpus delicti*, these interpersonal relationships are imperative, here and everywhere, for the formation of the ultimate showroom superstar.

Speaking of the latter, winemaker Scott Shirley came to Justin with 13 vintages under his belt and a purebred pedigree that included six years as enologist at Opus One and seven years at the Hess Collection where he specialized in mostly-Bordeaux blends like the silken 19 Block Cuvee, which contains an elaborate blend of grapes that includes syrah.

Very non-Napa-esque, but quite Paso Robles, where stirring in a little syrah to pinot noir is not only heard of, but actively bragged about. So, Shirley is delighted with the opportunity to stretch his stylistic muscles, and has fit in seamlessly here.

"I like to use cabernet in broad brushstrokes," he relates, "then soften or amplify the edges with blenders. Virtually every finished wine is a ultimately a blend of one kind or another, whether of clones, varieties, barrel types or vineyard sites."

Here, the crucial collaboration involves Grower Relations & Estate Vineyard Manager Paul Kaselionis. *Terroir*, top to bottom, is his territory — a bailiwick he loves. Having graduated Cal Poly with a degree in Agribusiness Marketing and Wine & Viticulture, he learned the school's signature hands-on approach to wine growing, which he has translated to a love and respect for local vineyards.

So, when the moon is in the Seventh House and Jupiter aligns with Mars, the fruit of labor and fermenter is presented in style within Justin's glossy design-statement, Zen-modern tasting room equipped with a California-cute and eno-able pour staff.

The work-horse cash cow wines that retail at around $25 are

ripe and sharp, nice Paso precedents.

Isosceles, the paradigm, is rich and ripe with black cherry, exotic spice, cedar, eucalyptus, graham cracker; all those complex things you expect in a $60 premium cab.

In a hundred dollar ultra-premium cab like Isosceles Reserve you demand it, of course, but according to Gerakaris, the wine is allocated so anally that you have to know somebody to get it...

Which is not entirely true, since I know somebody and didn't.

Regardless, the Justin tasting room is decked out with splendid vineyard views through massive windows and like any self-respecting profit center, Circle K to Harrods, it is scattered with rocking little tchotchkes — Justin glass bung paperweights, Laguiole corkscrews, lavender vanilla honey, Elemental Herbs sunscreen and — lest you forget for a cocaine heartbeat that you are in California and nowhere else — gluten-free organic vegan trail mix.

But Jim Gerakaris steers me toward another product that, on the surface, seems just as California koo-koo, but on second glance, is pure, pimped-out Paso:

Late-harvest olive oil from Kiler Ridge Olive Farm, several miles up the canyon road. That I sort of have to follow up on, and like an accommodating sommelier might call a drunk a cab, Jim is kind enough to call Kiler Ridge and set me up for a visit.

Thanks, Jim. All that Fiji stuff is water under the bridge.

GOOD TO THE BONE:
KILER RIDGE OLIVE FARM

'There is even a greater degree of skill required in preparing oil from olives than in making wine from grapes,' said Pliny the Elder in AD 78, speaking about a frantoio.

And what's a 'frantoio'? A wrong turn if you don't speak Pliny palaver.

Turns out that it is a word used colloquially in Italy to indicate a place that presses olive oil, but when I see the sign reading 'Frantoio' with an arrow pointing left, I assume it's just another mom 'n' pop shop, this one owned by Mom and Pop Frantoio. So I turn right.

And wind up in the middle of a silvery-gray olive grove laden with rich, violet-colored, sweet-smelling fruit, a few thousand trees spreading around me. Like grapes, they love the searing heat and calcium rich soils of Paso Robles; they grow slowly here as they do in the Mediterranean, and like grapes, they produce better, more concentrated fruit when they struggle to survive through drought conditions. When conditions are correct, they are almost supernaturally long-lived, too:

There's a gnarled old fellow on Crete — The Olive Tree of Vouves — that is estimated to have begun life a millennia before Christ was born. Trees two thousand years old are not unheard of, which means that the very same trees that Pliny the Elder described above in *Naturalis Historia* — the encyclopedia upon which all other encyclopedias have been based — might still be producing fruit today.

Meanwhile, a considerably younger dude on the tractor directs me toward the frantoio.

And such a frantoio! A frantoio's frantoio — a frantoio among frantoii. Owner Gregg Bone, wearing a 'Bonecrusher' tee-shirt, is squat, powerful-looking from shoulders to waist and a bit of a schlub the rest of the way down. He is right in the middle of harvest, and so his obliging nature in taking me on a tour is worth the few moments I have to wait so that he can tie up some loose ends.

Besides, it gives me a minute to survey the remarkable building.

Constructed of rice straw bales (a waste product of California agriculture) sandwiched between concrete layers, the technology is an intriguing — if centuries old — alternative to wood frame construction. Besides being rot and termite proof, it is an effective, fire-resistant insulator and as Gregg points out, when the big earthquake hits, "Bale houses will be the last ones standing."

Gregg was an engineer in the real world, and his techie whiz-kid wizardry is everywhere. Garrulous and geeky, he warns me that a 'full-bore' tour of the facility can be taken literally and will take an hour and a half.

I scoff, of course, since there is nothing but olive trees and a press on the premises and how long could *that* take?

Ten minutes after showing off his skills as a stainless steel welder and detailing the precision that went into the software that coordinates the weigh scale via a wifi computer that controls the hopper and runs the mill that he designed ('Sometimes,' he laughs, 'it's good being a geek'), he begins a fifteen minute apologue about the blackboard in the mill-room (it has Lionel Pauling's fingerprints on it, he claims), I see that it will indeed be an extensive afternoon.

Here's the Cliff's Notes version of the blackboard story:

Thirty years ago, as a California Institute of Technology student, an old laboratory on campus closed down — one in which Lionel Pauling, the Nobel Prize winning chemist, had once lectured. Bone saw the 'keep out' signs as a challenge to his dexterous engineering fingers, broke in and stole the board, which he now has scribbled over with graphs and percentages related to olive oil production.

As to the nutshell version of that process, per Bone, producing artisan late-harvest olive oil — my *raison d'être* for interrupting Gregg's six-week-long harvest — requires picking the olives when they are completely purple-black ripe, even darker than the ones I'd seen when I drove in.

Ideally, oil olives are picked while still green, upon the cusp of maturity and about ready to go black and never come back — the stage is known in olive farming, as it is in vineyard management, as 'veraison'. At this point, their phenols — those aromatic, alcohol-like base compounds which olives produce to warn away bugs and birds — are at their highest. These have been absorbed into the meat of the drupe throughout the season, transforming into polyphenols, which are prized for their antioxidant properties.

Olives crushed and pressed at this stage develop a characteristic pungency and bitterness which may be better for our health, but worse for our palates. A blend of green olives and reddish olives that have begun to pass through veraison are often the best compromise to produce oils that are both heart-smart and delicious. Those left to fully ripen, harvested 'late', make oils which are lower in antioxidants, but are sweeter, less sharp and more complex in flavor, as is proven during our subsequent sample side-by-sides.

But first, note that here the emphasis is on 'oil' olives, a world removed from olives grown to be cured and served at the table.

In fact, admits Bone, "My olives are horrible to eat — they're greasy and cloying. The only person ever able to choke them down has been my mother-in-law..."

...A story upon which Bone chose not to elaborate.

In the end, it's the dipstick level. The ideal oil olive has a fat content of around 35%, while for table olives, best is about 15%. Thus, logically, table olives make lousy oil olives:

"All the work for half the output," is the way that Gregg Bone states it.

In either case, handpicking is pretty much a given when harvesting olives. The risk of damaging fruit is too great to trust mechanics. The slightest bruise or flesh wound introduces bacteria and may promote fermentation that will mar the purity of flavor that is the hallmark of artisan oils like Bone's.

Harvest season in the ripening groves may last a month or more, but once picked and separated from the tree's umbilical cord and access to nutrients, the fruit 'dies'. For the resulting oil to achieve the chemistry required to be genuinely labeled 'extra virgin', it has to be picked and processed within twenty-four hours. And that's a do-or-die opportunity window for Kiler Ridge.

Fortunately, unlike wine grapes, olives for oil travel along a streamlined flowchart. From the harvest baskets, they are quickly weighed and washed in a sort of cold-water Jacuzzi that gently agitates them, then dries them — the less water that is introduced at any point during the operation, the better.

The grinding step, which reduces seed, skin and olive meat to paste is done in a glorified garbage disposal, a 12,000-watt brobdignagian compared to the lilliputian InSinkErator that's probably in your kitchen.

Oil is contained within the vacuoles of olive cells, and thorough crushing tears the fruit apart and facilitates its removal. In days of yore, this was done with stone mills, and of course, in the rural Mediterranean, some are still in use.

Malaxing is the next vital step, and to no one's surprise, that's done inside an apparatus called a malaxer.

When first released from olive cells, the oil droplets are cell-sized, and too light to float to the top of the paste.
Malaxer is French for 'knead' and that's what happens within the mixing tank. In fact, Gregg Bone jokes that his malaxer could double as a bread kneader — only once, because you could never get it cleaned it afterward.

Americans may be willing to spend $100 on a liter of artisanal olive oil, but Gregg is pretty sure they won't spend $30,000 for a loaf of bread — which is what he'd have to shell out for a new machine.

From there, a powerful centrifuge acting on the principal of a salad spinner pulls the lighter oil to the center of a cylindrical tank, leaving some of the water and most of the pomace behind.

Given time, this separation would have happened naturally, as it does with cream and milk, but time is the x factor that the olive oil producer does not have.

Thinking like a true outside-the-box Trekkie, Bone envisions a spacecraft faster than light-speed transporting the pulp to

Jupiter, where the extra gravity could duplicate the earth-bound process — and then he woke up. This stage was traditionally done in a press, leading to the now somewhat-antiquated term 'cold press' and 'first press'. For the sake of modernity, 'cold press' indicates that the temperature of the oil never reaches more than 89 °F; much higher, before or after bottling, and the product rapidly deteriorates.

The oil then moves into a faster centrifuge which removes the remaining water, leaving oil and the few, nearly microscopic mites of vegetable solids into a large storage tank; gravity takes care of any further sedimentary fining that may be required.

Throughout the afternoon, Gregg Bone portrays olive oil as a largely misunderstood commodity, especially in the United States, and most of that misunderstanding works in the favor of giant industrial fat producers like Bertolli and Philip Berrio and against the little guy who does stuff right.

And most of what he says about the globalization, corruption, and outright fraud within the industry scares the bejeebers out of me. It's like taking a graphic, hand's on tour of a poultry processing plant: Guaranteed that afterward, you'll swear off *arroz con pollo* for a long, long time.

In the first place, the United States is not a member of the International Olive Council, which sets standards for more than 98 per cent of the world's olives, and so, we are not beholden to its classifications — including 'extra virgin' oil. And even so, adulterated olive oil is biggest source of agricultural fraud problems in the European Union.

In 2011, UC Davis tested 134 olive oil samples from California retailers, including seven popular imported brands like Filippo Berio, Bertolli, Pompeian as well as the top-selling domestic label, California Olive Ranch. Of them, 73% failed the smell and taste test standards set by the Madrid-based IOC, while chemical analyses gave failing grades to about half.

California oils fared far better, where growers have adopted a voluntary set of criteria established by the California Olive Oil Council, which meet or exceed the European standards.

Certainly, Gregg Bone's late-harvest, extra virgin olive oil wears the COOC 2013 certification seal.

'The first oil of all, produced from the raw olive, is considered preferable to all the others in flavor; in this kind, too, the first droppings of the press are the most esteemed, diminishing gradually in goodness and value', said Pliny the Elder in the same tome referenced earlier.

Picked and nibbled directly from the tree, an olive is an organoleptic train wreck. The unripe green ones that wind up as buoys in your martini glass are bullet-hard and physically impossible to chew — they taste like they've been marinated in boiled earwax. Ripe — as edible as they'll ever get without curing — they turn the creamy texture of an avocado, but still taste like they've been dipped in that hellacious liquid my mother used to paint on my nails to keep me from biting them. And, in fact, among the yucking-tasting compounds olives produce is oleuropein — the base chemical in that that very liquid.

Birds are wise to this natural defense mechanism, and won't touch olives.
A bit of bitter remains behind in very pure, freshly pressed olive oil, giving it a characteristic bite that may be so pronounced that it is actually difficult to swallow without coughing.

Bone's oil, as it pours from the final centrifuge and is captured in a paper specimen cup, has this quality. Fluorescent green, tinged with golden glitter and tiny flakes of olive particulate, his dreadful drupes have been coaxed and coddled, manhandled and manipulated from a nasty little nub of astringent ick to miracle grease.

It's a safe bet that whichever Canaanite first recognized the intrinsic treasure hiding within bitter olives, as well as the strange method of oil extraction upon which most of Mediterranean culture has depended for the last six thousand years, he must have been a clever fellow with a lot of spare time on his hands.

Clever DNA certainly seeps through Gregg Bone's system as well. Forget the seventeen companies he's founded, forget the Apple stock and the fortune he made during the dot-com bubble of the late nineties. Nothing tops 'Samuel Clemens Day' at Kiler Ridge Olive Farm:

That's the day that he solicits friends and neighbors for help in harvesting. And what does he pay? Please. He *charges* you to pick for him, thirty for adults and twenty for kids as young as five! Of course, lunch is provided. If you don't get the Sam Clemens connection, check out *The Adventures of Tom Sawyer*, Chapter Two…

…Wherein you'll see that Gregg Bone has managed to out-Twain Twain.

CHARACTER, IDENTITY & PURPOSE: TABLAS CREEK WINERY

It's the house that Hass built—namely Robert Haas, the exclusive American importer of Château de Beaucastel via Vineyard Brands, which he founded in 1971. This not to say that he didn't have a *foudre* full of help from Jean-Pierre and François Perrin, proprietors of Beaucastel. But when the two distinguished wine families first conceived of tracking down a California property that could not only match the Mediterranean climate of Beaucastel, but the high pH soils which bask beneath it, they didn't figure it would take a decade.

More to follow, but first, I will refer you back to Gary Eberle's grandiose and offbeat declaration that Paso Robles does not contain 'enough limestone to make a bag of cement.' Never so brazenly has the expression *'a picture is worth a thousand words'* been rewritten with an addendum:

'Especially if some of those words are horsepucky.'

Turns out that there's plenty of limestone in Paso—a solid wall of it in, fact—right outside the Tablas Creek tasting room. Robert's son Jason Haas leads me to it in order to show off the water-retaining ability in the sites lithographical makeup, allowing dry-farming on the estate's 120 acres. The wall—an ancient marine embayment—is improbably friable; a slab cracks off easily into his hand with a puff of white smoke.

He pours water from a hip flask on it and as I watch, the water is sucked—imbibed, ingurgitated—into a million microscopic pores.

"Technically, this is not yet limestone," he confesses, "it's calcareous clay stuck at a midway point without having seen sufficient heat or pressure to form solid rock."

To illustrate, he knocks the broken chunk against a boulder of the real deal, and the piece he's holding crumbles into water-dampened dust.

"You can't plant in solid limestone," he says. "Too hard. You have to catch it before it forms or after it has decayed. There's not much of it in Sonoma or Napa, but at Châteauneuf-du-Pape, it's bedrock."

The famed names of Southern Rhône rear up frequently in Jason's banter, and understandably so: As a younger man (he's still in the literal blush of youth, as his lean physique and full head of ginger hair may attest) he spent summers schlepping at Château de Beaucastel.

And this leads us back to the Haas/Perrin partnership: Believing that the decayed limestone beneath their classic *lieu-dit* has the ability to semaphore certain mineral qualities to the wine as well as soak up moisture, they searched all over California to find the precise combination of soil and sun, elevation and air and whatever *je ne sais quoi* French people believes makes this wine worth two hundred euros and the one in the vineyard next door, fifty.

They didn't expect to find it here, and had begun the search where Rhône varietals had seen some previous success, and barring that, they looked at appellations where zinfandel had produced its richest incarnations—essential zins that could display both power and poetry.

Zinfandel, they reasoned, was the genetic equivalent to Croatia's crljenak kaštelanski, which grows best in the precise conditions they wanted.
And at that time, in California, zinfandel had a far more

impressive pedigree than mourvèdre or rousanne. And so, finally, they came to Paso, where they were delighted to discover their beloved limestone in a narrow crescent a few miles from the ocean, where tectonic pressure had caused the Pacific seabed to crumple upward rather than subduct beneath the mainland, bringing to the surface all that pretty, moon-white, New World calcium.

Sonoma County tends to contain a lot of igneous, granitic and quartz-rich rocks while Napa is more volcanic in origin. Paso once resembled Puget Sound, with shallow ocean life living in large estuarine systems, which were later, pulverized and crushed into rock and clay by the inexorable grinding of the continental plates.

Once the Haas/Perrin team settled on Paso Robles, the search began for property, which had not been previously farmed with pesticides and synthetic fertilizer, because they didn't want to inherent toxicity with the contract. The plan had always been to hit upon a California microclimate reflecting Southern Rhône's, and after a decade of due diligence and cash saving, neither partner was willing to settle for less than the real estate mantra: *Location cubed.*

The master plan involved dry farming a fully organic vineyard and planting cuttings from Beaucastel, and this was a fairly ambitious bucket list, but ultimately, on an old, west side alfalfa farm, they found everything they wanted. Days were hotter here than at Beaucastel, and nights were cooler, but when you did the math, the average temperature was nearly identical. And here, the rains held off an extra month compared to France, not putting on a serious show until mid-November. So that allowed the grapes the extra time required to develop the sugars and acids to become what viticulturists call 'flavor ripe', when the grapes begin to bag out and the seeds are allowed to fully lignify.

A further rain-related slice of kismet blesses these vineyards:
Situated about halfway between Paso Robles and the Pacific
Ocean at an elevation of about fifteen hundred feet, they see as
much as twice Paso's annual precipitation totals due to ocean
dumps which rarely make it beyond the mountains. Without
this liquid manna, dry farming would not be possible, even
with the spongy, pervious calcareous soil.

Now, here's a disclaimer: When the man says 'dry-farmed', do
not get the impression that Tablas Creek vineyard managers
never water any vines ever; nobody with the aim of remaining
in the grape business during droughts says 'dry or die'. In
fact, they say the opposite, and if they claim otherwise, they're
probably lying—it may be stating the obvious, but without
rain, bragging about dry farming is silly, because it becomes
more a handicap than strength. Newly planted vines need
water, and if older vines need more than nature is willing to
provide, they don't provide for the farm—they buy it.
The trick is to irrigate as judiciously and sparingly as is
consistent with healthy plants. Not often—maybe twice a
year instead of every couple weeks—because roots learn to
expect such pampering and hang toward the surface to await
the hose.

Left to their own devices, however, they burrow deep, and the
big root mass winds up in the limestone layers, not in the
topsoil, and the deeper they go, the more nutrients they find.

This is the point where wine grape horticulture deviates from
nearly all other forms of commercial agriculture, where the
eye is upon the fat yields and copious crops; with wine
grapes, your goal is not necessarily to play nursemaid to your
charges, but to coach them—to set excruciatingly tough
parameters and push them to the ragged edge of their
capabilities.

To produce wines of quintessence, you don't indulge them.

You train them to ride the Tour de France.

2013 wound up being the quickest harvest in Tablas Creek history—44 days from start to finish. This was the result of the shrewd training regimen as well as dumb luck. According to Jason Haas, throughout the summer, west side Paso hill country enjoyed a fortuitous ripening season without rain, heat spikes or frost.

After finding their Shangri-La, the second major waiting scourge that Team Haas and Perrin endured was the UC Davis quarantine that their important Rhône cuttings had to pass. And in the worst case, such legally mandated disease prevention may take a decade.

The young vines are tested for various viruses—petri dish work, to be sure—and nobody is allowed to plant anything without their clean bill of health. In general, the wait is well worth it, especially when you insist on planting untried varietals that nobody else around can sell you—like Haas/Perrin did. Wandering the grounds, for example, I see grapes rarely, if ever, found outside of France—picpoul, clairette and especially picardin. In fact, the half acre of picardin that Tablas Creek has planted effectively increases the world's picardin population by 50%: France grows only a single acre's worth themselves.

One of the biggest surprises that Haases and the Perrins encountered were that their white wine grapes—primarily rousanne, marsanne, grenache blanc and viognier—were far more nuanced and consistent than they had expected. This was due to the Paso pasturage, unique unto itself no matter how hard they tried to channel Pope Jean XXII, founding Father of Châteauneuf-du-Pape.

And as they came to grasp the potential of these grapes in

140

Paso — as an American extrapolation of French theories — they could not help but notice that most of the clones that other earnest California Rhône buffs grew were substandard. A wine's obligation is context; it should acknowledge its surroundings.

That's ultimately a winemaker's magic, but when it comes to what leaves the ground compared to what goes in, the old data processors cliché — Garbage In, Garbage Out — holds true.

A less magnanimous and more avaricious vintner might have gloated over the Tablas Creek foresight, but as a board member of The Rhône Rangers since 2008, largely responsible for shifting the focus of this Northern-based educational group to the Central Coast, Jason Haas — who sells everything he makes anyway — stumbled into the nursery business, educating his fellow growers on the best raw material to further the Rhône Ranger's mission of raising the public's appreciation of these wines in Americanized couture, then selling it to them. In total, Jason estimates that he has provided ten million cuttings to more than six hundred West Coast vineyards.

Once crushed, the juice is fermented in separate lots — blending waits until Spring, when the character of each vintage's varietal becomes less murky and options are greater — and whites and reds are kept in separate areas, like boys and girls in Muslim schoolrooms, to offer individualized temperature nurturing to each.

GIGO may apply to barrel philosophy as well, and the textural character of wood and its influence on wine is perhaps better understood at Tablas Creek, and monitored more closely, than in any other winery in Paso Robles. Massive, French-made *foudres* holding 1200 gallons hold twenty times the volume of a standard barrel line the cellar. The overall contact between wine and oak is proportionally reduced; juice is tinged, not torpedoed.

This works particularly well for white wines, and it's here that the Beaucastel tradition strays from form.

To me, and likely to you, the innovation seems so tiny as to be essentially unworthy of mention, and is done so only because Jason Haas reported it with unbridled delight.

Having worked beneath a Perrin shadow in Rhône and being clever enough to neither wish to be nor have the constituents to be a Beaucastel knock-off, he glows with pride as he shares the fact that after he blends the grenache blanc with the rousanne, it goes back in the *foudre* for another spell of stave brooding.

"We were the first to oak it after blending; the French would *never* do that."

As such, the tasting room becomes not only a sales vehicle, but also a synthesis of themes.

Like many wineries of the scale and scope of Tablas Creek, where interlocking varietals of varying oomph and vintner care equate to different price points, the essential system of release is in three tiers, each one showcasing a concept and, to some extent, paying homage to the strengths of a favorite clone.

The spectrum of aromatics rising from a glass of wine can either prove the taste or send it back for rework. A wine's scent — it's most complex sensory submission — should be a barometer of its flavor, adding a gloss of certainty to what we already smelled.

There are cases where a given wine surprises, and even shocks by delivering to the tongue a gamut of goodies that the nose failed to hint at, but these are rare. But smells are volatile, requiring warmth: The wines of Tablas Creek, even the reds, are presented chilled, mimicking what the Rhôneish *vignerons* consider 'room temperature'.

I thought they were too cold and sometimes blunted the taste and highlighted tannins in the reds and muffled the bouquet in the whites, but then again, what do I know? I'm not a Rhôneish *vigneron.*

Anyway, that's why God gave picky critics sweaty, overly hot palms that are fully capable of cradling a tulip glass until it warms up.

The entry-level wine goes under the label Patelin, French slang for 'country neighborhood'. It sells for around $20, and is the only non-estate wine that Tablas Creek produces. In order to oil the machinery of a 25,000 case winery, tender at this price point is pretty much a stipulation; most Paso winemakers would love to market a low-end, populist beverage if they could. And Patelin shows itself as such. It's a workhorse wine that plugs along without dreams of winning a Derby. The white is about half grenache blanc, the rest an amalgam of viognier, rousanne and marsanne; the red, from 14 nearby vineyards, most planted with cuttings sold them by Tablas Creek, is a mix of syrah, grenache, mourvèdre and counoise.

Next up is the Cotes series, which demonstrates a bit more determination and specificity. The red is a rhythmic and textured mingling of the same classic quartet, with a bit more emphasis on grenache and counoise.

The white pushes back the grenache blanc in favor of spicy, pear-rich marsanne, and floral viognier, adding compelling perfumes and better structure.

Tablas Creek's flagship wines, Esprit, further move the needle, both in mouth and at the cash register. Patelin is good, but this is the difference between B-roll and boom mike.

Manicured, bouncy and propulsive, it is the house blend that most nearly replicates the ratios used several time zones away at Châteauneuf-du-Pape—the closest the winery can come to a tribute. Trusting heavily in mourvèdre, in the highly rated (94 in *Wine Advocate*; 93 – 95 in *Rhône Report*) 2010 version is one-third grenache, 21% syrah and 4% counoise. It's a satisfying wine, to be sure, but lacks the bravura of its parent. Without the density, force or gravitas of Beaucastel, Esprit manages to echo much of that wine's legendary elegance with a bit less of its earthy transcendence.

In all events, I believe that Jason Haas has a good sense of the magic he is weaving within his stand-alone interpretations of traditional blending grapes, and if he doesn't, he should—mourvèdre especially. It is approached with almost mythical reverence, but equally, with analytical clarity; Haas relishes in the grape's unquenchable exuberance and understands that Mourvèdre is what makes Beaucastel Beaucastel. It stands to reason that it would be trademark Tablas cultivar.

Of similar authority is his rousanne. Here's a grape that a had a fairly embarrassing California mis-introduction in the 1980s when Randall Graham, Bonny Doon's periphrastic winemaker, smuggled in cuttings from Châteauneuf-du-Pape (he claims) and sold them to several cult wineries, notably Caymus. In 1998, DNA analyses revealed that the cuttings were actually viognier instead of rousanne—not exactly the same as discovering that your prince is really a pauper, but a '*Doh!*' moment nonetheless.

Tablas Creek rousanne is rubber-stamped 'fraud free', registered authentic and certified clean by the State of California. On the vine they are russet-colored and redolent, and in the bottle they reflecting that grape's complex skein of aromatics and fruit-salad versatility.

"Rousanne is a tough cookie in the field," says Jason Haas. "It ripens late, has poor wind resistance and uneven yields. It's prone to powdery mildew and oxidizes easily. But if you can deal with that, it becomes a pliant baby in the cellar. You can do with it what you want."

One of the things he wants is the sort of dessert wine made in climates without noble rot, without December deep-freezes, and indeed, the grapes proved eager to play.

'Quintessence' is produced as a warm climate answer to ice wine, *vin de paille* — 'straw wine'. The technique is so labor-intensive that hardly anyone bothers — it involves drying grapes on racks covered with straw until they raisinate; without water, the juice becomes concentrated with esters and glucose, resulting in a sappy but stately wine which (in the best) sidesteps syrupy with a judicious spritz of acid.

And 'Quintessence' is every bit of that. Alongside the expected notes of dried pear, honey and apricot, there is a prominent and delightful note of maple candy.

In fact, Tablas Creek's unblended mourvèdre and unblended rousanne are among the best wines I tried in Paso Robles. They are the rare bird that seems to have entirely grasped its raw material in context of a new terroir while paying proper homage to its history. It's like a Frenchman who, after years of expat living in the United States, retains only a slight accent.

But, the accent is there — subtle, genuine but unmistakable. As Jason Haas points out, "It's nice to have a partner who's been making wine for a hundred years."

THE TERRIBLE TWOS

Tear gas, water cannons and rubber bullets won't work. Tasers, electric batons, sleep deprivation and hanging-them-by-their-feet is useless. So, Steve Thompson has been known to sit in the canyon opposite his vineyard, drink a bottle of wine and unleash live-fire hell upon the ground squirrels.

He's also developed a sort of John Wayne vs. the Injuns technique while driving his red Polaris wherein he steers with one hand and fires his shotgun with the other. In either case, on a particularly productive whack-a-squirrel day, he may send three hundred rodents into oblivion.

Whether or not you experience convulsions of conscience over such wanton rodenticide probably depends on how you earn your living.

Squirrels are not the vineyard only scourge, but they are the only one without a natural predator beyond coyotes — which local ranchers have a tendency to use for target practice also.

Importing live coyotes is another option, and however silly and ironic it may seem — carrying coals to Newcastle — but with California tightening birdshot laws, it may become inevitable. He quips that if he could find an upscale market for squirrel meat, like The Abalone Farm has for mollusks, he'd be able to pay off the mortgage in a season.

Of seasons, he's seen fewer than most of the earthy, gray-bearded proletarians I've run across. In fact, 2007 was his first vintage, when a bumper crop and high prices put smiles on the faces of every grower on the Central Coast.

He'd spent the previous twenty-four harvests at sea with NOAH as a ship captain, working with fisheries and as part of port security. Medical issues prevented him from any more ocean duty, and perhaps fortuitously.

As he puts it: "By then, I'd grown tired of D.C.'s bureaucratic bullshit."

Several years ago, along with his twin brother Stu, Steve purchased 45 acres, of which 32 acres were already planted to vineyard — although, since then, he has grafted a lot of it over to varietals he prefers. Most conspicuous among these is petite sirah, for which he finds his sandy loam and moderately low rainfall ideal, and also Stillman's pet varietal verdejo — the only notable quantity of verdejo to be found in Paso Robles. The farm is relatively flat, sitting at about 700 feet of elevation — another plus, he says:

"Easier to irrigate, easier to harvest with a more even yield of fruit. You tend to get a lot of ripeness variation in mountain grapes, and I've seen growers swear by grades that turn the harvest into an extreme sport."

Sitting outside the mobile home he occupies during harvest, Thompson's eyes dart back and forth — vivid watchfulness that probably suited him well in the Coast Guard on a coast where drug smugglers have been known to ply and fly.

He's a tall, handsome, normally taciturn man that is doing things the way he wants to do them. He likes the idea of sustainable agriculture, but he's not beholden to organics or dry farming. He irrigates when and however much is required.

This year, for example, he's seen six inches of rain instead of the customary sixteen, making him luckier than many who have been dealing with less than two. Nonetheless, it hasn't rained since January, and his drip-hoses are out in force.

He's a supporter of sustainable farming systems that are biologically based — the 'whole farm' approach to vineyard management, where cover crops and composts are preferable to chemical fertilizer. Which is not to say he does not use them when indicated. In fact, this year's petiole (leaf) analysis determined that his tank was low on nitrogen, phosphorus and potassium and he topped off the acreage with equal parts of each.

He also machine harvests his crop, something that is only possible when the slopes are not extreme. These days, high-tech harvesters can be programmed for individual vineyard blocks and eliminate the need for crusher/stemmers. Besides, with immigration turning the screws and a shortage of labor, it saves him the headache of having to hunt down field hands. In the long run, he asserts, it is cheaper to pick mechanically anyway. It's same sort of shotgun pragmatism that puts the ground squirrels on notice.

Of course, with the *Spermophilus beecheyi* (a name so funny, I cannot resist using it), he has traps and poison and smoke to work with as well. Says Steve: "I've seen ground squirrels kill a vine overnight, then get up in the morning, eat the grapes and chew through the irrigation pipes."

Gophers are less of a problem, because Paso's several species of owl — especially the Great Horned kind — feature them on the menu; the early bird may get the worm, but the late one gets the rodent. Steve's acres are ringed with owl boxes, each one painted with a warning to tractor drivers to drive slowly and not raise owl-disturbing dust while during nap times. A slightly different technique is required for starlings and similar grape-greedy game like finches and robins, which can wipe out a vineyard over a weekend. Solutions range from pricey polyethylene netting (making harvesting tough) to bargain-basement Mylar strips (a fusion of The Scarecrow and

The Tin Man) which in theory startle starlings with reflected light, but in reality, once invading birds become acclimated, sort of don't.

Periodic blasts from air cannons work, but tend to annoy the non-agricultural neighbors, if that sort of thing is important to you. Another problem with this method is that the birds return fairly quickly, so you have to keep up the barrage throughout the day. Same goes for recordings of raptors — birds of prey — loosed at intervals at low-rider woofer levels.

With a nod toward the sanctity of ecology, organic farming and silence, the fix that best fits may be hiring companies like Atascadero's Airstrike Bird Control. They refer to their service as 'bird abatement' and for a substantial fee, they will dispatch a falconer and one or more falcons to your vineyard to patrol for roving bird flocks. It is expensive, but cost-effective for vineyards of four hundred acres or so.

According to Steve, who tried it once as an experiment, "For two or three days, the falcons do their thing. After that, the arrival of the truck itself is enough to scare the birds away. They are programmed to fear falcons — that's an evolutionary accommodation that doesn't apply to buckshot or Mylar."

Larger vineyards have indeed begun to favor falconry; the complaint I hear from smaller growers who can't afford the service is that the frightened starlings often wind up on their grapes.

Might be a last hurrah for the Trickle Down Theory.
I missed Stu Thompson the morning I met with Steve — he was in the wine warehouse, boxing-up cases of syrah from the brothers' label, Twin Coyotes Winery, which will be sold as bag-in-the-box at a local wine bar. This is, in fact, the one and only time I encountered bagged wine in Paso.

Proving what? That the brothers are not only thinking outside the box, but inside it as well.

RE: RE:FIND–
A RE:MARKABLE FIND

If Alex Trebek posed the answer *'The smartest guy in Paso Robles'*, what would your question be?

The more I think about it, the more I figure that mine would be: *'Who is Alex Villicana?'*

Some Rhône-focused winemakers use a Spanish technique where they bleed juice from the vat after crushing the grapes and allow the leftovers to macerate with double the volume of skins, thus concentrating available phenolics. The loanword used is *paso doble* — Spanish for 'double pass' — and the extra juice is considered superfluous and usually dumped.

Suppose you walked into the brainstorming session at the winery — in this case, I promised not to name names — and said, 'Not only have I figured out how we can avoid pouring out all that watery, thin juice down the drain, I found a schmuck *who is willing to pay real money for it.'*

Would you be the smartest guy in Paso? Nope. You'd be the schmuck who sells thin, watery gold to the smartest guy in Paso:

Alex Villicana.

No rational businessman likes to waste product, which is where petroleum jelly comes from: It's essentially the waxy residue that occasionally has to be removed from oilrig pumps. And was simply trashed until 1873, when Sir Robert Chesebrough refined it and renamed it Vaseline.

Ah, that word: Refined. Or, Re:Find.

Since opening the doors to 13-acre, 1800-case Villicana Winery in 1993, such cavalier wine wastage rankled Alex Villicana. I mean, it stuck in his craw like a sliver of French oak.

He says, "The free-run juice can be made into saignée rosé, but not very good saignée rosé; if you're going to make a pink wine, you grow, pick and vinify for that. Sugars are too high in our bled juice, and the wine winds up pretty flat. I don't want my name on that."

Still, pouring it into the irrigation reservoir is not an appealing alternative — it smells yucky and attracts fruit flies. Why it took nearly a quarter century to figure out that you could make moonshine out of it may be another Jeopardy answer, but it did. In any case, Re:Find Distillery opened two years ago, and has been a success nearly worthy of the knighthood that Robert Chesebrough received in 1883 — upon which occasion Queen Victoria extolled the product's usefulness, claiming that she 'used Vaseline every day'.

That's a quote I will not touch, except to say that a few shots of Re: Find might have greased her skids even better.

The first year, Villicana turned a thousand gallons of surplus saignée into 200 cases of liquor, and knew he was onto something big when he sold out immediately. So, the following vintage he began to nose around comrade crushers to see if they could be convinced to sell them their garbage at a premium price.

Rhetorical question, evidently. Last year, when the brainchild was barely into toddlerhood, Villicana peaked at ten thousand gallons of what has been described as 'amazingly alluring' by *The Tasting Panel* and went for the gold in Martha Stewart's 2013 Audience Choice awards.

A few re:marks on Re:Find's routine:

The fact that our word 'alcohol' is derived from the Arabic كحل (al-kuḥl) and first distilled by Islamic chemists — a faith that bans its consumption — is ironic. Distillation involves heating a fermented liquid to a point above the volatility of its alcohol content (172 °F) but below the 212 ° required to vaporize its water content. The cooled, re:condensed steam contains ethanol — the stuff that makes us dance on bar tables, streak football games, sing karaoke and propose to people we just met — along with other lower-boiling-point impurities like methanol and acetone.

Because both of these undesirables evaporate at a temperature even lower than alcohol, they end up as the first drops in the collection vessel. The wise distiller throws these away; the unwise distiller has a seeing-eye dog — as little as 10 milliliters of methanol can cause blindness. These are called the 'heads' of distillation. The 'tails' are the heavier fusel oils like butanol (paint thinner) and the absurdly named furfurol, which causes an explosive furfurol free-for-all if allowed to get too hot. Traces of each remain, so, if the liquid is put through the process again, a more pure — and hence, smoother — *eau-de-vie* emerges. The theory is that by the time you have done this an infinite number of times, you are left with a substance that is, by definition, perfect — pure ethanol, without taste, color or odor.

The concept of perfection, of course, is unachievable. In his treatise *Metaphysics*, Aristotle described it as '*that which is so good that nothing of the kind could be better*', which is why distillers keep on keepin' on.

Funny thing is, the imperfections that don't kill you — called congeners — are what give grog its persona; strip them all away and you are left with what the United States Alcohol and Tobacco Tax Bureau defines as '*a neutral spirit distilled from any material so treated as to be without distinctive character, aroma, or taste'.*

In other words, vodka.

A key misconception about vodka is that it is necessarily Russian or Polish in origin; that it made from grain or potatoes — and that each brand has its own identity beyond marketing shtick. Note that the TTB specifies that *vodka qua vodka* (more Aristotlese) should have nothing within its essence that detracts from its neutrality. If it is not intentionally flavored, one ideal vodka should taste exactly like any other ideal vodka, which is to say, like nothing at all. As such, it can be made from anything... rye, potatoes, beets, lawn clippings...

Or Paso Robles saignée.

With the sun on a downward arc, lighting the late September hillside with glints of gold and russet, Alex Villicana looks simultaneously relaxed and hyperkinetic. He's a handsome guy in the sort way that gets instant approval from the girl next door's mom; he's a marathon runner and it shows. He waves a hand toward the slope, where the vines are in process of their summer sayonara.

His harvest has been in for a week, the grapes crushed and fermented (primarily grenache, mourvèdre and syrah), and the first step of distilling — he calls it the stripping run — has begun.

"One distinct benefit of grape vodka," he says, "is the compound glycerol which is produced during the fermentation. It forms the 'legs' in a wine glass and has a sweet, viscous quality that gives liquor uniquely smooth, soft characteristics."

This is true grape brandy, and cannot be confused with the kerosene-like grappa distilled in Italian farmhouses. Grappa is not made from grape juice but from grape pomace — the leavings of a winemaking operation — and distilled dry by employing steam via a *bain-marie*-type gizmo.

Villicana does it the way they do it in Bavaria, with a Holstein copper vertical still. This is a sparkling spire of form-follows-function engineering and a beautiful thing to behold.

Yet, though the elixir that dribbles from the business end is truly magnificent, it does not get passing grades on the TBB's vodka exam: It's anything but neutral. Bubbling throughout the spirit's intoxicating infrastructure are fleeting floral flavors and a rich, almost oily concentration of citrus and vanilla as well as the striking scent of...wait for it... *lawn clippings.*

Gentle and gentile at the same time.

And then there are the cucumbers. Seasonally, Villicana will infuse his vodka — Russian, like *eau-de-vie*, for 'water of life' — with various organic delights, and on the day I stop in, it's ripe cucumbers: An effortless indulgence and an unalloyed triumph.

Villicana offers artisan gin as well, and the macerated blend of coriander, orange peel, lavender, grains of paradise (an African spice related to ginger) and orrisroot is a velvet wash across the tongue.

To figure out how to make such a silken purse out of saignée sow's ear requires a new breed of radical, an auspex on the advance guard of the alcohol army.

How cutting-edge is Villicana's Re:Find?

Put it this way: If the *Double Jeopardy!* clue is *'As of September, 2013, the only craft distillery in the entire Paso Robles AVA'* — consider yourself a shoe-in for the cash.

Bo Barry & the Dark Side of the Moon

Ol' Bo wants his city back, and brother, is he determined to get it — and ol' Bo doesn't care how vocal he has to get about it.

I call him 'ol' Bo' despite the fact that he's fit and 32. I have no idea what his real name is, and maybe that's it. But to me, 'Bo' sounds like an old person's handle — Bo Diddly, Bo Schembechler; Bo Jackson is over the hill and Bo Derek's cornrows have turned gunmetal gray.

And don't get me started on Bo Peep — she can't keep track of sheep let alone her age.

Speaking of sheep, Bo Barry is as dyed-in-the-wool Paso Roblan as anyone in town; other than a few years in Florida, he has pretty much always lived here. His mother ran a day care in the center of town and throughout his life, he's been exposed to a broad sector of the local rug rats, many from working class homes and grounded in the sort of keepin'-it-real worldview that Bo idealizes to this day.

The year he was born (1981) was the same year that Justin and Deborah Baldwin founded Justin Winery, and Justin's 2010 purchase by an L.A.-based billionaire may be a metaphor for the Paso Robles wine industry's unbridled growth over the intervening decades.

When Bo was a baby, there were only eight wineries in Paso; it was not yet an officially recognized AVA and the 'heritage' grape was zinfandel — fat and happy in the blazing heat of San Luis Obispo county.

Baldwin and a few others pioneers like Stanley Hoffman and Gary Eberle thought the microclimate perfect for a Bordeaux-style blend, and within a decade, Tablas Creek visionary Robert Haas and his partners, the Beaucastel brothers Jean-Pierre and François Perrin were planting Rhône varietals in the arid, high-elevations.

They were outsiders, but they were able to adapt to the indigenous culture; to contribute to it, to enhance it, to fuse with it: They were to the community what merlot is to cabernet sauvignon. In short, they were as respectful to their new neighbors as they were to their new geology.

Then, the rest of the world got the memo.

"All of the sudden, the wine business exploded," Bo remembers, and not fondly. "Great for the city's economy, great for them. But instead of becoming part of Paso Robles — a real storybook small town, where people were always there for you, where cops stopped to help you change your tire, where we didn't need curfews — Paso Robles sort of became part of them and their culture. As a community, we became overrun with egos. With arrogance and a sort of rich-kid attitude. "

He points to the loss of the West Coast Kustoms Car Show, which had hauled cash and cars from all over the world into downtown Paso for thirty years, as a watershed moment: "The wineries didn't like the cruise and the show; they complained about the noise, the trash — claimed there was gang vandalism, people pissing on lawns and so on. I remember it being family-oriented, rockabilly bands, something we looked forward to as kids."

To hear him tell it, the city fathers — ultimately, the folks responsible for deep-sixing the lead sleds, hot rods and nifty fifties festival — are all in the pockets of the wineries.

And, since the three day Memorial Day throw down was not necessarily wine oriented — rod freaks tend to be more a Bud Lite crowd — it had to go, along with the other loud and lusty local lollapalooza, the Tattoo Expo. It drew ten thousand people to downtown Paso every year, he insists, until the *think drink, not ink'* dinks dumped it down the sink.

"It was a monster hit in its first year," he declares. "Upwards of ten thousand people showed up. As a concert promoter, those are unheard of numbers for an event with no major bands headlining."

Bo is, in fact, a concert promoter — according to his business card he is Creative Director of MCC (Music of the Central Coast) and CEO of Blitz Entertainment Group (BEG). His business plan involves developing, packaging, booking and promoting the homegrown talent until the Central California music scene is as juggernaut an enterprise as the wine scene.

It sounds like a tall order, but there is a sort of unstoppable quality about Bo Barry; he's like those beanstalk beans that Jack threw outside his window — plant a seed in his brain (in this case, 'What's wrong with Paso Robles these days?), then run like hell, because he will race-walk talk without pause for as long as you'll let him — until the cows come home, literally.

Because the Paso he pines for was populated by a lot of cattle people, and he shakes his head at least a couple of his friends, ranch kids, who used to tug on Durango shit-kicker boots and who now slip into $500 Gucci sneakers.

He reserves the same sort of shuddering scorn for local girls he grew up around who now work in winery tasting rooms or serve wine at fancy dinners and who — in his opinion — are putting on airs. And Bo has laser vision when it comes to bullshit:
"This isn't Hollywood and we shouldn't want to be

Hollywood. This isn't even Napa. Paso Robles is a sleepy little cow town with remarkable vineyard soil, that's all. I knew these girls when they were eating corndogs at the California Mid-State Fair, when they had friends of all kinds, African American, Hispanic, whatever. Now—and I hate to say it—they look down on hard-working, blue collar Mexicans. I've seen them give me dirty looks when they see me with my black brothers. Like, I know who you are, girls—I grew up with you. That made-up glamor and so-called class and rudeness ain't you. It ain't in you, because you weren't raised like that."

And to the guys in Guccis: "Dudes, you're cowboys. You look like a bunch of hip-hop thugs. You are supposed to handle these kind of things with dignity."

Bo looks like Eminem, and part of that is calculated—the backward Dodgers cap, the oversized t-shirt, the close-cropped brown hair—but most of it is not. Like Slim Shady, Bo Barry looks out at the world with a sort of steely, half-quizzical glare, neither threatening nor particularly friendly. And, like Marshall, he is far smarter than his persona radiates and fiercely focused to a point where speaking to him can be a bit off-putting. If I was a betting (and stock-buying) man, I'd invest in MCC—if he has half the drive and moxie in that endeavor as he did in my interview, it'll be a hit.

Like all successful entrepreneurs, it's not necessarily the self-confidence he feels, it's the self-confidence he telegraphs. He contacted me three times after our interview to mention other non-wine events that used to be part of Paso's heritage but have been killed by (in his opinion) the bought-and-sold city council:

"We had the Amgen Tour of California bike race, too. Lance Armstrong was here along with all those low-flying helicopters and news vans like you see on TV. It's gone, too, for some undisclosed reason. But, we know the pattern already, so we didn't need a reason.

And later: "Oh yeah, I almost forgot about the Digital Film Festival; it brought superstars like Clint Eastwood and Gary Busey to town. Five days of events. Benford Standley was the organizer; he'd arrange for a lot of permits and everything and they still jerked him around."

Okay, so admittedly, Bo Barry may be infected with the 'conspiracy theory' bug that has essentially replaced democracy as the motivating force driving American political commentary. He is extraordinarily worried about radiation from Japan, the imminent declaration of martial law, and he believes that organic cooked vegetables can heal cavities and that he has a colorful 'aura'. To his credit, he is equally amenable to admitting he's wrong when I send him interesting Snopes links about these topics.

Over the years, I've noticed an innate paranoia that seems to be part of the id-package of children raised in single parent households without a lot of cash. Some of these kids are hell-bent on proving that they have little to offer the planet, and others are equally determined to explode from status quo and kick the planet's ass.

Bo is of the latter breed. He posted a question to his Facebook friends on Paso's decline, Mayberry to metropolis, Main Street to mean streets, and within an hour, he got dozens of replies from Paso contemporaries who were in full agreement. The advent of a drug culture, even among elementary school kids, watered-down morals, an uptick in racism and crime and a general feeling of disquiet is there now that was never there before.

How much of this is directly related to the wine industry is debatable; Bo's sincerity about bringing back Paso's Norman

Rockwell charm is not. And somehow, I trust that, even if he doesn't succeed, he's going to die trying.

Just as I trust that when he gets to the top of his beanstalk, he's going to discover that he was the Giant all along.

THE NUTCRACKER'S SWEET

I wound up in Paso Robles wine country instead of any other wine country partly because when I mentioned it to a friend, she asked, "Is that in Texas?"

Not only that, but I seriously didn't even know how to pronounce it: I said *'Paso'* with an 'ah' and *'Robles'* with an 'ace' as if the citizenry still pronounced the city like the Spanish Catholics did.

Besides, Paso offered perfect fundamentals for my scope: Promise, past and pioneers with pizzazz, many of who are still alive and interviewable. I loved the idea that the appellation is hovering between old school and new wave, ingenuity and institutions, and I was curious if in real time, the balance is tilting on the tightrope and about to pull a Karl Wallenda, landing on one side or the other, or if the current crop of vintners are eager to preserve Paso's delicate twoness. And I was intrigued to discover my idealized Roblan, with textbook texture and an eye on the rearview, both outside of and directed by history, was not in the vineyard but in the walnut grove.

Jutta Thoerner is proud of her nuts, and justifiable so. They are small, thick-skinned beauties, able to withstand the tribulations of dry farming while scrabbling into the kitchens of a wider audience.

In fact, when it comes to their caretaker, the nut doesn't fall far from the tree.

Since purchasing two hundred acres in the Adelaida Foothills in 1992, Jutta — and her partner Cynthia — forged a mission statement that has not fluctuated a whit:

"We wanted to obtain organic certification; we wanted to be able to sell walnuts retail, not wholesale. We did not intend to, and never have, employed fungicides, pesticides, synthetic fertilizer or hormones on the farm. Ever."

And they were willing to embrace all the associated and unanticipated headaches: As we tour the orchard, for example, Jutta crooks her thumb at a National Geographic-quality live trap in a small clearing between orchards.

"Wild boar," she indicates. "Not as big a problem as squirrels," she maintains, "but when one shows up, you better believe he can eat more than a squirrel."

Ground squirrels, the Biblical plague of California produce growers, are rife in this part of western Paso, and Jutta points out a neighbor's distant walnut farm on a hillside above Adelaida Road. "For a number of reasons, he failed to set traps this year. The squirrels took over, it was like watching the frogs overrunning Egypt — it was creepy to watch from here; the whole ground looked like it was moving. Last year, when he set traps, he harvested 25,000 pounds of walnuts. This year? Zero."

A single squirrel, she tells me, can eat $50 in nuts per season. That cannot be in any rational farmer's business plan, of course, so for abatement, she relies on traps, traps and more traps. And esurient coyote. Like Steve Thompson of Twin Coyote Winery, she shakes her head in muddlement at local farmers who kill them.

"Why not just shoot yourself in the foot and save ammunition?"

Yet to Jutta, even more frustrating than these raptorial ranchers and rapacious rodents are consumers who neither grasp nor care about the effort required to earn and maintain 'organic' certification in California.

More than once, in the course of the interview, the wry, grey-haired fireplug made sure I understood that *that* was her message; *that's* what she wanted people to understand.

Under Title 21 of the 1990 Farm Bill, in order to label your product 'organic', you have to comply with principles and authority of the Organic Foods Production Act, primarily insuring your use of materials and practices that enhance the ecological balance of natural systems and that integrate the parts of the farming system into an ecological whole.

In abbreviated form — something at which the USDA does not excel — organic farming is based on an agro-philosophy that calls for maintaining healthy, living soils; the primary focus is feeding the planet, not the plant. Do *that* right, the theory goes, and the plant will take it from there. This includes managing the property without pesticides or synthetic fertilizer, relying on compost, organic manures (animal and 'green') and avoiding excess tillage. Whereas there are specific federal standards and guidelines for the production of certified organic crops, the overreaching rationality of organic farming often extends to a social conscience as well and it is fair to say that organic farming owes as much to moral commitment as to physical compliance.

The bureaucracy, of course, doesn't care whom you voted for. The bureaucracy cares — demands — that you keep careful records, including historical documentation of farm practices while undergoing routine checks by government-approved inspectors.
They'll show up at random and sniff around the farm, the farm records and your farming practices. Extra care is taken

to ensure that you have not used irradiation, sewage sludge, synthetic fertilizers, prohibited pesticides and genetically modified organisms; nutrient sources are given a microscope by the Organic Materials Review Institute to ensure standards compliance.

As you might imagine, for a two hundred acre farm with a hundred acre of walnut trees primarily managed by two women with day jobs, the paperwork required to cling to that precious seal is daunting by itself.

And it's not like they're raking in the dough along with the walnuts. On the contrary, their prices often follow a market dominated by mass-produced, heavily irrigated walnuts from the Central Valley that have been bred for numbers, not nuances.

She shares scare-stories about techniques used in the quantity-is-king commercial walnut industry, which are often bleached for appearance and fumigated with fungicide. Major growers often harvest walnuts before they are ripe and, in order to 'cook out' the resultant rubbery texture and 'green' flavors of these nuts (and extend the shelf life), they may be heated to extremely high temperatures, destroying much of the buttery sumptuousness that is telltale in walnuts that have followed nature's timetable. By contrast, Jutta's nuts are never dried at temperatures above 85°F — often lower than the ambient air. Also, in order to maximize output, commercial growers plant trees in huddled masses ten to fifteen feet apart. Optimum spacing for organically dry-farmed, low yielding walnut trees is about thirty feet — and harvests are reduced accordingly.

"Organic farming is a war against doing business as usual," Jutta explains. "We see higher production and labor cost, which makes operating the farm challenging. But we are hopeful that raised awareness will lead to increased demand and, over time, support organic products at prices that are recognized as appropriate for the value received."

John steers his tractor to a likely target—a walnut tree that is heavy with fruit and ready to drop. This is neighborly synergism at its finest; John owns the tractor and Jutta owns the tree shaker.

Re-bar thin, with a Mr. Green Jeans affability that's revealed when he removes his dust mask for a photo op, John extends the shaker's boom arms around the tree trunk in a horticulture hug and locks it in; the apparatus is equipped with eccentric weights, and it's brief moment of glory, makes the tree look like a wet dog drying off.

The entire enterprise, shuddering, convulsive and remarkable, takes about four seconds; roughly the same duration as the 2003 San Simeon earthquake.

And the nuts—nearly all of them—drop to the ground. Now comes the human touch, pain in the ass though that touch may be.

Since the nuts must be gathered within a few hours of harvest—twenty-four at the most, otherwise they can fall prey to pest infestation, discoloration or mold—a hired crew is required to do what Jutta admits is 'horrible, back-breaking work'.

The only thing harder, she says (and as Emiliano has previously attested), is picking strawberries.

Mechanized sweepers are used by the big boys in Central Valley, but Jutta has had bad experiences them; along with the nuts, they suck up a lot of sticks and stones, which can indeed break your bones—or at least, the bones of your husker. And husking is next critical step in preparing walnuts for market.

The one used at Manzanita is a set piece from a Historical Society exhibit. Seventy years old, jury-rigged with baling wire, louder than a shuttle launch, the gas-powered monstrosity winds up being very efficient at remove the bittery green husk from the nut in a very simple tumbling operation through something that looks like a big, cylindrical cheese grater. From there, the nuts are slowly dried, and thus, are made pretty for the masses.

At one time, Jutta was one step beyond these masses; before she'd streamlined her process and did the math, she sold her walnuts wholesale, where commercial processors would do some of the dirty work, including hulling and drying.

Problem is, industrial-level producers couldn't care less whether the nuts are dry-farmed or raised without synthetic crap, and an organic crop winds up in the warehouse along with everybody else's. And they pay the same rate regardless, sometimes as little as a dollar a pound, at which price the whole dry farm experiment becomes not only illogical but also impossible.

Jutta may be nuts, but she's not crazy. To her, this was a case where Diamond was not a girl's best friend.

But if Diamond is the enemy, that's 'enemy' with an asterisk, and the century old company deserves kudos, certainly.

Founded in 1912 by a cooperative of Californian walnut growers, Diamond became the first nut company to advertise nationally, the first nut company to recognize the potential of television commercials and, in fact, their Super Bowl XLI spot featuring Robert Goulet was ranked as that event's number one ad by Advertising Age and resulted in a 68% sales increase for the brand.

Clearly, Diamond of California has worked just as hard for

their portion of patrons as Jutta has for hers.

Like her nuts, Jutta's audience may be smaller, but it is far more rapt. Why? And *why walnuts?*

In part because walnuts have been heralded as a near-perfect food since Alley Oop was king of the jungle; they predate the last ice age as a nutrition-dense staple of the human diet, and by 5000 BCE, evidence shows that they were being cultivated by Neolithic people in the Mediterranean. With the rise of Rome, they became an indispensable trade commodity, and amphorae filled with walnut residue have been salvaged from sunken Roman ships. Besides being delicious, the kernels were used extensively as medicine, said to cure everything from baldness to upset stomachs.

And speaking of the Romans and their painful abdomens, the next time you refer to your testicles (providing you have them) as your nuts, thank Jupiter, king of the Roman pantheon. The scientific classification is *Juglans regia*, Latin for 'The King's Gonads'.

The Greeks apparently thought that a walnut looked more like a head, but I simply refuse to go there.

As a food source, walnuts are high in protein and fiber and possess a unique fatty acid profile, and compared to other commercially produced nuts like hazelnuts and almonds, have a higher concentration of free antioxidants and antioxidants bound to fiber. Ironically, black walnuts — to which Manzanita Farms was originally planted — offer more of all the above, and in better ratios. But they are notoriously hard to process: According to Jutta, "You have to take a sledge hammer to them to get them open."

So she replanted with heirloom English walnut trees like Franquette and Hartley, known to bear nuts with exceptional and distinctive flavors, nuances like butterscotch and a sort of creamy sweetness that lingers in the aftertaste. In this, and in the stress-factor of cultivating in rough soil without irrigation, there are plenty of parallels to winemaking and wine tasting. English Walnuts are fairly easy to grow provided you have time—a tree requires seven years or so from seed to set, and after that may produce two tons of nuts per acre each year for upwards of half a century.

With dry farming's requisite tree spacing, Jutta may only see a half-ton per acre, but all the taste and health plusses are mustered within the meat, and so far do they surpass what is available at the grocery store that you'll need to swallow some to swallow their superiority.

She's not out-fashioned by technology, she's elevated by purity of mission—and by the majesty of the endgame. If California is regarded as growing the world's top-quality walnut (99% of the commercial US supply; three-quarters of global trade) and if Manzanita Manor produces the finest walnuts in California, a first-year student of transitive relations can write the equation.

Yeah, That Paderewski...

In you are not from Paso Robles, the 800 lb. bronze statue outside the Carnegie Library in Centennial Park may offer a WTF? moment. It depicts bushy-haired Ignacy Jan Paderewski, the Polish composer and diplomat whose best known works include *Minuet in G, Op. 14/1* and the lyrical drama *Manru*, which is the only Polish opera ever performed at The Met.

Paderewski was born in 1860 in the village of Kurilovka (then part of the Podolia Governorat) and died in New York in 1941; Chicago's Polish Museum of America contains most of his artifacts, and his body — originally interred at Arlington National Cemetery in Virginia is now buried in Warsaw. Unlike Tony Bennett's, not even his heart is in California — for some bizarre reason it is encased in bronze and sits inside a church in Doylestown, Pennsylvania.

So, why the Roblan monument?

It turns out that if Sesame Street ever did a show on Ignacy Jan, it would be brought to you by the letter 'P' — that bilabial plosive seems to have stalked the composer's bio like a moonstruck groupie. Paderewski was a popular Polish pianist from Podolia (his mother's name was Poliksena); as a politician he became Poland's Prime Minister and perorated pompously at the Paris Peace Conference in 1919.

And then there's Paso.

In January, 1914, with Europe on the brink of World War I, Paderewski bought a 2000-acre spread (Rancho San Ignacio in honor of the saint whose name he shared) just west of town. This was huge news—at the time, Paderewski was the world's most famous pianist, bigger than Liszt had been fifty years before; according to a *fin de siècle* article in Etude Magazine, he could readily command $7000 dollars for an hour-long performance—$175,000 in today's bucks.

Paso Robles, by contrast, was a backwater whistle stop between L.A. and San Francisco; the 1910 U.S. census lists the Paso population at 1,441. Setting up shop in the Adelaida Hills would have been the equivalent of Lady Gaga building a recording studio in Possum Trot, Kentucky and making moonshine on the side.

It was the clean hot springs that attracted him—Paderewski suffered from career-threatening arthritis and was big on sulphur soaks—but ironically, it was the dirt that kept him. As a diplomat and world traveler, he'd been exposed to some of the finest wines of his era, and decided that the handful of then-available Paso wines had the potential to equal them. Thus, Paderewski became the 'p' word that has the most significance to this piddling pandect: A pioneer.

Among those Paso people who have more recently had this plaudit pinned to their *pechos* by Parker Jr.—John Alban, Stephan Asseo, Justin Smith, Robert Haas—not one was so much as a glint in the old man's eye when the pianist planted his first vine cuttings.

Like many of his modern counterparts, Paderewski had contacted the University of California for viticulture advice, and having surveyed the land, Professor Frederic Bilotti recommended petite sirah for the eastern slopes and zinfandel for the highest elevations.

So, that's exactly what Paderewski did. And yet, by all accounts, his early wines were disappointing, and by the time the virtuoso V.I.P-cum-vintner contracted York Winery to craft his I.J. Paderewski label, both were already comfortably settled into middle age.

Hand-built by Indiana native Andrew Jackson York from wooden beams from a dismantled Cayucos pier and bricks he formed and fired on the spot, Ascension Winery had begun producing wine in 1882; he changed the name to reflect the family patronym when his sons came on board.

York's commercial success attracted not only his kids, and within two years, the Ernst family arrived from Geneseo, Illinois and expanded the portfolio of Paso plantings to 25 varietals. In 1886, Gerd Klintworth moved north from Orange County and released the area's first white wine, a sweet and potent concoction called Angelica. Frenchman Adolfe Siot remained on the zinfandel bandwagon, and the winery he started in 1890, now owned by the Rotta family, is producing old vine zin to this day.

Other nineteenth century trailblazers include names that still appear in Paso Robles' White Pages—Casteel, Nerelli and Anderson—and many are still in the wine trade. But York Mountain—now owned by Epoch—lays claim to be the oldest continuously operating winery in the Central Coast.

The York/Paderewski collaboration was golden. Literally: In 1934, the year after Prohibition, I.J. Paderewski Zinfandel took top prize in its class at the California State Fair.

History and hooch notwithstanding, the short, winding drive up York Mountain Road—before Highway 46 was built, part of the lone conduit between Paso Robles and the coast—is a trip worth taking.

As a congenital Midwesterner, I find myself tree-starved in much of central California, and the undulating path beneath a canopy of ancient oaks and pines, punctuated by grove-filled gulleys and occasional vistas, is balm in Gilead.

The hump of hill country upon which York Mountain Winery sits was hit hard by the 2003 San Simeon earthquake of 2003, but despite catastrophic damage to the structure, the winery was hit even harder by debt.

And that's thanks to (former) owner David Weyrich, who the Cal Coast News excoriated in a 2009 article entitled '*How to Lose $200 million in 10 Years*'. Having sold the family business for $600 million in 1998, the aptly-named Weyrich took his share and went on an epic buying spree; beside York Mountain Winery, he picked up a company that leased business jets, a luxury bed and breakfast, a hotel, a yacht and, in general, lived a life of such as would have put the flamboyant, often over-the-top Ignacy Jan Paderewski to shame.

And shame indeed wound up being the name of the game. In 1999, he founded a chain of newspapers meant to reflect the community's 'family values'; in fact, he used it an outlet to promote his anti-gay rights agenda, and a year later, after his staff jumped ship, it folded.

All told, in all his diverse endeavors, he defaulted on tens of millions of dollars in loans, some from family friends and long-time associates, and his assets — listed in 2007 at $70 million — were liquidated on the San Luis Obispo county courthouse steps in 2010.

At the time, no public mention was made of the fate of York Mountain Winery, but Epoch soon released a statement saying that the landmark business was theirs.

If you want to interview Epoch owner Bill Armstrong, you'd better be prepared to take some licks. Bill Armstrong is a licker by inclination and a licker by trade, and it is hard for him to describe the sense of awe he feels every time he strolls through his vineyards without picking up a chunk of siliceous shale from an outcrop and slobbering all over it. He'll urge you to do the same, and licking it *is* pretty remarkable: So porous is the cream-colored rock that your tongue sticks to it, sucking up saliva like a Hoover upright and effectively preventing you from physically interrupting Armstrong as he launches into a long, long geology lesson — thus, there's method to his madness.

This kind of stone, you will learn, is formed over millions of years as globular radiolaria plankton die and form a glassine pile on the ocean bed 'like a stack of miniature billiard balls'. Apparently, as they decay into silica-rich ooze, their skeletons remain somewhat intact, forming microscopic air pockets that, despite the passage of eons, remain in rock formations and sponge up moisture — even tongue moisture. Siliceous shale is California's answer to licking a Michigan lamppost in January.

"It's a unique depositional deposit," Armstrong claims. "There's a lot of calcareous shale here in Paso, but not as much silica. These are the kinds of soils you find in Priorat, Spain; these are soils that cover half of Bordeaux, and — most intriguing to me — pockets of land in Southern Rhône."

Big, bald, brash and brainy, Armstrong is a Denver-based geologist with a peerless palate and a penchant for Pape. While studying stones at Southern Methodist University in Dallas, he was bitten by the wine bug, and found that the big, bold, brash and beefy wines of Châteauneuf-du-Pape were a personal favorite. User-friendly, often high in alcohol and always booyah charismatic, these wines are regarded as among the best in France.

Armstrong, while inveigled by the flavors, was not intimidated by the reputation:

"At the time, I was broke as a joke," he laughs, both wistful and amused at his own chutzpah. "I had no cash, no vineyard, no knowledge of winemaking, but I knew enough about lithology to believe that if I could find the right soil with the right elevation, the right exposures, the right diurnal shifts, there would be no need for me to mimic the masters. I could make a better wine in California than I could in the Rhône Valley."

And so, along with his wife Liz — also a geologist — the search began for a California site with all the 'x factor' ducks in a row and all the stars aligning overhead. It was a long and arduous task, undertaken on foot, at the library, and by tasting the multitude of West Coast wines with the sort of organoleptic profile the Armstrongs were after.

And, finding a region to fit the bill was, perhaps, the easy part. They also had to find a specific *lieu-dit* within that region, and it had to be for sale, and they had to find a local whiz-bang willing to act as a consultant.

Enter Justin Smith.

"I wanted to enlist Justin's considerable talents — I was in love with his Saxum wines, and needed that kind of expertise to help me choose a site, advise me on grafted root stock, to help me make the kind of product I was visioning."

He cold-called Smith, whose reticence is the stuff of local legend — I tried for a month to set up an interview with him and had no success. He was willing to meet the Armstrongs for coffee, and as Bill tells it, "He only said three words during the whole conversation. Two of them were 'Oh' and the other, a very low-key and unconvincing, 'Cool'."

But Smith was impressed enough with the Armstrongs' game plan that he agreed to become part of the site search, although Armstrong confides that his ultimate choice of property met with more than a little skepticism. "I knew it was perfect, that I had stumbled on one of California's sweet spots — rolling hillsides, high-lime calcareous clay, and most importantly, siliceous shale. Justin sort of shook his head when I said, 'This is it', and that made me trust him even more. He had every reason in the world to encourage me to buy land out here — I was offering him a job."

The fact that this sixty-five acre vineyard — nicknamed 'The Rewski' by Justin Smith, was the same land that Paderewski had planted eighty years before was an interesting plus, but not by much — by his own admission, Armstrong didn't know Maestro Ignacy from Cagney & Lacey. But he was quickly brought up to speed, and today is quite a repository of rapid-fire Pad trivia.

The Epoch team planted in 2004, a mix of classic Rhône grapes and tempranillo from Rioja, and five years later, with the release of 2007 the plums and plaudits started piling in. Say what you want about the validity of the hundred-point scale, if your first release pulls down 90s from all the major publications (including a 94 from both *Wine Spectator* and *Wine Advocate*), you may claim your bragging rights. And they've gone right on claiming them.

Justin Smith now wears the badge of 'consultant' while Epoch's new winemaker, Jordan Fiorentini, upholds the prize-winning tradition begun by Paderewski — the 1920's version of a rock star — and maintained by a geologist Bill Armstrong — a twenty-first century *real* one.

When it comes to pronouncing foreign words, Roblans tend to be practical, utilitarian — even hardheaded — even their beloved, lyrically named El Paso de Robles winds up as *'Paaso Row-bulls'*. So, I imagine that they are having a collective field day when discussing the annual Paderewski Festival, where, for a two hundred dollar V.I.P. pass, you can buy more vowels in four days than Vanna White has sold in her lifetime — with a few consonants thrown in *gratis*, including an 'f' to replace the second 'w' in Paderewski.

For example, in 2013, the headline performer was Karol Radziwonowicz, the first person in the world to record all of Ignacy Paderewski's music. Violinist Pasha Tseitlin played chamber music while Krzesimir Dobski played jazz.

A film by Wieslaw Dobrowski chronicling the composer's life was shown; Marek Zebrowski presided over the Youth Piano Competition, at which point, they must have run out of letters: The Legacy Award went to a boy named Lin and First Place by a boy named Ha.

Easy for you to say.

But, in the end, how easy was Paderewski to drink? I'm reminded of the adulation still paid to the opera world's first diva, soprano Anna Renzi, even though no living soul has ever heard her sing. For all we know, she could have sucked.

Throughout the time I spent in Paso, I tried to find one person of any age, who had actually seen — let along sampled — a bottle of I.J. Paderewski Zinfandel. I mean, the man died in the '40s and President Franklin D. Roosevelt presided over his funeral arrangements, referring to him as 'a modern immortal', so it stands to reason that someone, somewhere, had the circumspection to squirrel away a few cases, for its auction value alone if not for posterity. But, I came up empty — even Hy Blythe, 90, a local history buff and the man who commissioned the eight-hundred-pound bronze gorilla in front of the library, had never even seen one.

So in the end, all the Paso praise piled upon Paderewski's plonk is evanescent homage paid to a dream.

Or is it?

Somewhat late in our interview, Bill Armstrong brought up his odd, but for the sake of this story, significant find.

When installing a deer fence at the periphery of his Paderewski acreage, he discovered a single vine that had been missed by Prohibitionists, ignored by subsequent owners and the ravages of time and had no doubt been planted by Paderewski himself. It struggled at the base of a hill, tangled among the trailing purslane and furry hedge nettle, gnarled and gnarly, defiant and thirsty. He's pretty sure it's zinfandel, not petite sirah as UC's Frederic Bilotti had recommended for this elevation, and there are cuttings now being analyzed for DNA. Whatever the outcome, Armstrong intends to recreate the sort of wine that the old prize-winning Pole could have actually produced here.

It will be merely a model of the original, of course, a superficial semblance of the real deal, like the statue outside the Carnegie Library in Centennial Park is to the man himself, but you know what? Scroll YouTube until you come up with the 78-rpm recording that Paderewski made in 1937 of Beethoven's Moonlight Sonata. It may be scratchy, filled with static as and dusty as a vintage bottle from York Mountain's cellar--but damn, the colors he draws from the instrument! His subtle, majestic phrasing!

Here's hoping that the next generation of Paderewski's zinfandel proves to be an experience as moving,

FOSTER'S FAT-FILLED, FUSS-FREE FAREWELL

Most food and writers search for superlatives. Runners-up tend not to keep the interest of either scribe or scribee.

But if I had a hamburger for every bold opinion-maker who claimed that so-and-so's freshly-ground, ramped-up Wagyu beef burger could blow everyone else's out of the tub, I could feed Ethiopia for a week. And if I had a Mason jar of rotgut White Mule backyard moonshine for every 100-point wine that was really, truly without a single imperfection (as the word is literally defined), I could keep that same country cockeyed for another week.

Most food and wine writers search for superlatives and never find them. I certainly found no such absolutes in Paso Robles, nor did I really expect to, but what I did find was far more absorbing and adjective defying and, perhaps, just as unexpected.

It was in the blood and not the bottle.

A parade of beguiling characters are dusted throughout the spare and spacious vistas of San Luis Obispo County and many define the notion of character itself. Each one has his or her own personal creation myth; his own *savoir-faire*, her own temper spreadsheet. They are shape-shifters in the sci fi sense; some come with winemaker stains, some in dirty dungarees, some in black tees with pentagrams, some in Stetsons, some in embroidered ecru paisley blouses.

These gonzo geeks and boho rebels may have stolen center stage in this story because they are each superlatives in their own dimensions, but, I have no doubt, a cast of equally charismatic performers is waiting behind the scenes, just beyond my feeble spotlight.

On either side of the curtain, each is making a path through a private maze of ambition and resignation, growing life by means and methods that may ultimately defy sanity, but not ecology — and crafting personalized oeuvres that breathe the sort of intangibles that get lost in mass production.

As an appellation in the aggregate, Paso Robles is welding one-of-a-kind wines, poised and luminous when the unique *terroir* is fully understood, rather limpid and shapeless when it is not. Like everywhere, I suppose, there are winemakers here prepared to dig a giant pit in the middle of the vineyard and shovel money into it so long as they can produce wines that flame with splendor; others are content to drink the grape Kool-Aid and ride the coattails of off-the-rack corporations bent on shoveling money out of as many pits as they can dig — no matter how many hundred-year-old oak trees they have to bulldoze to get there.

Conscience has never been a requisite, or a particular advantage, to fortune making. And that's an issue to the Paso pioneers, especially those who scrabbled through scrub and stone to build their vinous brainchildren into proud, earth-serving adults. Sure, it focuses an international laser beam upon their graphics, but that's not always the best prescription for a wine republic's reputation.

Witness Australia, where an ocean of streamlined, simplified seven dollar wine set supermarket shelves ablaze, leading to a consensus among many casual American wine drinkers that cheap and chillable is the proper Aussie profile.

Sales of charismatic, character-driven mid-range to pricey wines from Barossa and Hunter Valley began to falter and have not yet recovered despite the {yellow tail}-bashers among cognoscenti with access to a blog.

Paso's best value price/product wines may fit this upper-register parameter, and very few are cash cows.

There are cheaper wines, for sure, and the sweet spot in tasting rooms seems to be in the $15 - $35 range, which is what the vast majority of customers will buy no matter what is being poured.

But it may be fairly calculated that a $60 dollar bottle of Michael Gill syrah enjoys a smaller overall profit percentage than does a ten dollar bottle of J. Lohr syrah; such are the economies of scale. As Paso can produce hillside wines of magnificence and depth ('the steeper the slope, the better the grape'), it's also warm enough to make jammy, overcooked flatland wines by the lake-load (with a lake's worth of irrigation, of course) and sell them supermarket cheap.

And this, regrettably, may be part of the appellation's paradigm shift in years to come now that the largest winemakers find that they can move to Paso and produce millions of cases per years. For now, of course, it can be argued that so little boutique wine flows from the Paso pipeline compared to Napa and Sonoma that it sells out quickly — much of it to local businesses and the all-important wine clubs — and that there's no rationality to offering a sweet-spot wine for thirty dollars when it will sell for twice as much just as quickly.

Not only that, but if a mid-sized winery wants national distributorship eventually, they will have to extend deep discounts — up to half — to make it worth the corporate effort and keep the tariff consistent.

On my final night in Paso Robles, I wanted to meet up with

Bridget again, and I offered to take her to Foster's Freeze for a burger and a shake — not so much because I am a cheap bastard, but because it seemed like the kind of joint that generations of awkward, pimple-faced teenaged California dorks took their first date. As such, it might make an apposite milieu for what is likely our last date, since I have found that squiring small-town girls with live-in boyfriends around that same small town rarely ends well.

Foster's has been a real-life proving ground for hormonal adolescents since 1946; it's what Arnold's was to Ritchie Cunningham and what the candy store meant to that chick that fell for *The Leader of the Pack*.

I hope those kids made the best of these affairs in the timeless realm of puppy love, but they probably didn't. I hope that they fell head over heels and dug the time they were on their backs, and they probably did. But most of all, I hope that they were able to delay as long as possible the onset of grown-up cynicism; the conclusion that even the most romantic among us may finally stumble over — that is, in the end, the heart is a meat pump and not much more. Make whatever psychological or physiological mélange of that you like.

All I know is that tonight, no dice on Foster's. Bridget has undergone a California nutrition re-purposing. Not as extreme as that Masonic cult of dieters, vegans, but one which precludes hedonistic binging on grease and sugar such as teenage metabolism can withstand with no ill-effect (beside the aforementioned acne) and folks like us — at least those who give a shit — cannot.

Apparently, Foster's greasy, sodden sliders or a cholesterol-choked chocolate sundae do not fit the fitness bill, so we end up at Villa Creek, an upscale dining room that would not be out of place on Melrose Avenue or Columbus Circle.

It offers elevated takes on standards like tacos (with *crème fraîche* and mustard seed salsa and ceviche (with yuzu — a Korean orange) in suitably pricy and impractical portions that give you the impression that no matter how much you spend, you'll still be hungry when you leave. The food, what there is of it, is spectacular.

But, is it Paso?

Of course it is. There is a certain gentrified feel about downtown, notwithstanding the quaint central park and former library, now the Historical Museum, but the last traces of Paso's gritty past have settled pretty firmly into the earthquake dust. The only business that retrofitted following the earthquake were those who could afford to — the rest moved on. Many buildings are clearly new, and some are still undergoing transformations.

But wine is clearly the medium in which Paso Robles has re-invented itself, with numerous tasting rooms and wine-themed outlets, and it's no more alien to this environment than Fosters Freeze is, so I opt to do both.

Foster's alone, afterward, as the sun begins to plunge into the distant sea at the end of another bloodless, cloudless, balmy California day. People here assume that because I'm from gloomy Michigan I must love this weather, but come on, y'all — this ain't weather. This is non-weather. Tornadoes and blizzards are weather.

But I do get a twinge of guilt about thinking so, now a month in.

Because in a month, I have become as tuned to subtle changes in the weather as Michael Gill's shoulder: Breezes shift, thermals tack, temperatures may not plummet or skyrocket, but they vacillate with certain sophisticated delicacy.

And that's a metaphor that parallels the Paso Roblans.

You can write about people for years and never fail to be amazed at the leagues of depth that delve beneath a few millimeters of human skin. The delights and sometimes the depravities; the mosh-pit of righteousness and vulnerability. Among the spare and spacious vistas Of San Luis Obispo, I found them all.

Drunken homilies and alcohol-fueled anecdotes aside, there is a distinct Paso ethos — an anti-elitist view that at the end of the day, when the sugars sleep and the acids thrash and party, they are simply dirt farmers with a creative flair. Most approach their life's work as a homogenized nod to the workings of the planet and the workings of the mind, equal tribute to Newton and Darwin. Their passions are not unanimously obsessive-compulsive, but in the best exceed the confines of pure rationality.

Here, as everywhere, there are no pinnacles of art untethered to talent.

Those were the winemakers and wine drinkers that I had come to find, and amid, the miasma of mites and mildew, rainlessness and rodents, I found them in profusion.
Did I ever fit in? Not really, no more than I do at home perhaps, but after a month I was at least accepted. This is a fatalistic race, and under certain parameters — primarily respect for, and rudimentary understanding of this Paso ethos — they will accept. I became *'Oh, that wine writer who doesn't drink wine'* with all the attendant nods of sympathy; problem drinking is as rife here as it is anywhere, and a drunk is just an alcoholic that doesn't attend meetings. I was the dude with stones enough to walk into a saloon with a local loco with the platinum hair and lime-green toenail polish and was, by default, fly enough to not be cold-cocked with a

Louisville Slugger.   Maybe not 'one of us', but at least not 'one of them'.

One of *it*.

'It' has always been the intangible; the great voiceless, omnipotent void, the unreachable star for Quixotic questers, whether armed with lances, hydrometers, nutcrackers or Acer laptops. It is, of course, as elusive as the green flash in the sun as it settles into the Pacific.

But that's cool. After all, evolution is not in the finding, but in the rummaging.

Made in the USA
Middletown, DE
16 April 2016